TONALITY—ATONALITY—PANTONALITY

TONALITY
ATONALITY
PANTONALITY

A STUDY OF SOME TRENDS
IN TWENTIETH CENTURY MUSIC

by

RUDOLPH RETI

Author of "The Thematic Process in Music"

GREENWOOD PRESS, PUBLISHERS
WESTPORT, CONNECTICUT

Library of Congress Cataloging in Publication Data

Reti, Rudolph Richard, 1885-1957.
    Tonality, atonality, pantonality.

    Reprint of the ed. published by Macmillan, New York.
    Includes index.
    1. Composition (Music) 2. Music--Theory. I. Ti-
tle.
[MT40.R394T6 1978]   781.3   78-6162
ISBN 0-313-20478-0

Reprinted with the permission of Barrie & Jenkins

Reprinted in 1978 by Greenwood Press, Inc.,
51 Riverside Avenue, Westport, CT. 06880

Printed in the United States of America

10 9 8 7 6 5 4 3 2

This book is dedicated to the generation of young musicians today; for only through their creative interpretation can it attain its true meaning

AUTHOR'S PREFACE

THE following study was written within a few months. But its content developed as the result of almost a lifetime's search. Thus a few words about the idea which motivated the search may be justified.

This book is meant as a plea and stimulation for that part of the contemporary compositional endeavour which is outspokenly 'modern' in style, perhaps even radically modern, yet at the same time attempts to retain and renew the vitality of expression and human appeal that always characterized great music. In this sense the book may find itself somewhat in opposition to compositional manifestations derived from the concept of atonality and some techniques affiliated with it. But it will also, and perhaps even more strongly, be in opposition to those contrary tendencies that seek a solution in aesthetic eclecticism, in the necessarily futile attempt to fill old shells with artistic life. Instead, the book will set up an artistic goal of its own, neither tied to the rigidity of a new structural scheme, nor directed towards musical formations of the past. Though, therefore, the impulse behind the following deductions is an aesthetic and spiritual one, the presentation of this impulse may often inevitably assume a technical character. However, the reader will understand that the technical terms are merely formulations through which in the musician's vernacular the artistic and human ideas, which are the real issue in this study, can be more accurately described.

There is still one point which should be stressed from the outset, in order to avoid any misunderstanding. Although it is the purpose of this study to describe the evolution of certain *principles* in contemporary music, the following presentation will have to use works of individual composers to demonstrate these principles. Yet it should be understood that these composers are not introduced and discussed for their own sake as it were, that is, in order

vii

to evaluate their general artistic achievement, but only in so far as their work points to certain specific trends, the description of which is the goal of our explanations. Thus, if for instance a composer of the artistic magnitude of Strawinsky is discussed only with respect to one compositional aspect, the rhythmical, this does not imply that his creative significance is considered to be limited to this one sphere. Neither is any aesthetic evaluation intended if many widely acclaimed composers of today are mentioned only in passing or are not mentioned at all. This book does not purport to give a picture of the modern musical scene, but merely to demonstrate one of its specific trends, a trend which, moreover, only now begins to assume some clearly perceptible silhouette. Only what seemed to the author to be pertinent to this specific evolution—and he is well aware that even so his endeavour must remain very incomplete—was included in the analysis.

CONTENTS

ix

ILLUSTRATIONS

Twelve-tone or Twelve-Note

The term 'Twelve-note' was used in *Orpheus in New Guises* by Erwin Stein (Rockliff, 1953) in the passages translated by Hans Keller and in *Composition with Twelve Notes* by Josef Rufer translated by Humphrey Searle (Rockliff, 1954).

'Twelve-tone' is used in this book because that is how the late Rudolph Reti wrote it and an alteration throughout without the knowledge of the author might in some instances have implied shades of meaning which were not the author's, particularly in view of the main title of this work, which is being published simultaneously on both sides of the Atlantic.

—*The Publisher*

THE PROBLEM SUMMARIZED

AROUND the turn of the century the physical sciences, as is generally known, underwent an extraordinary change. Alfred North Whitehead, for instance, speaks repeatedly of the tremendous impression this great and almost sudden change made on his mind and views. About 1880 the laws of physics, as they were known then, seemed to represent something like an eternal truth, definitely established for all time. What remained to be done, said Whitehead, seemed to be merely the co-ordinating of a few newly discovered phenomena with the basic Newtonian principles. Then "by the middle of the 1890's there were a few tremors, a slight shiver as of all not being quite secure, but no one sensed what was coming. By 1900 the Newtonian physics were demolished, done for!"[1] However, even if the actual force of the old laws seemed to have vanished, their usefulness and validity within their own realm did not by any means disappear entirely. In fact, one main goal of modern physics seems to be centred on the endeavour to comprise and unify the old and new principles in one all-comprehensive law or formula.

The whole process, which is especially conspicuous in physics due to the paramount importance physical discoveries have assumed with regard to our material way of life, can also be observed in many other spheres, for instance in the psychological, the social and the political domain, and even in the arts, and particularly in music.

It is well known, not only to the musician but to every musical listener, that the whole set of principles which lay, consciously or instinctively, at the basis of all music from the so-called classic and romantic period (roughly speaking the period from Bach to Brahms and Wagner) began to crumble, as far as the compositional practice was concerned, in the 1880's or 90's. Consequently,

[1]Lucien Price, *Dialogues with Alfred North Whitehead*, Little Brown, 1954.

the music of the twentieth century, the so-called modern music, is in its whole concept of style not only different from but in some respects fundamentally opposed to that of the preceding centuries. This fundamental change was felt in almost all the various spheres through which the composer expresses himself, such as the melodic and rhythmic shaping, the thematic construction, the architectural patterns, even the instrumentation. But the most conspicuous, the most incisive change took place in the realm of harmony or, since harmony may in this connection be a slightly inaccurate term (and we shall return to this later), in what by a more comprehensive technical term is referred to as *tonality*.

Tonality, during its undisputed reign of several centuries, was so taken for granted and became so entrenched in the musician's mind as the natural, the 'eternal' concept of musical construction that when, because of its overlong use (and finally abuse) its abandonment became inevitable, the first slight signs of such an abandonment shocked the musical world to the core. From this fact a peculiar misnomer in terminology resulted—a misnomer of fairly far-reaching consequences; namely that to all music that did not fit into the customary and sanctified concept of tonality, the term *atonality* was applied. This term, however, was—at least at that time—a gross exaggeration. And today we would certainly not call atonal the music of, for instance, Strauss, Reger or Mahler, for which the term was originally often used, nor that of their French contemporaries, Debussy or Satie. Yet the term became generally accepted and although we would in our time discriminate more carefully between atonality in a specific, concrete sense and atonality as a general and vague idea, there is, even today, much confusion prevalent regarding this subject.

But there were more serious consequences involved than merely inaccurate terminology.

The abandonment of tonality, which in the beginning was but a slight deviation, became stronger and more violent year by year until in the so-called twelve-tone music even a learnable technique seemed to have been provided through which pure atonality, if one so wished, could be maintained in music.[1] The adherents of this trend towards outright atonality soon proclaimed their principles as the only valid ones, by setting up a kind of doctrine, a formula of evolution somewhat like this: "Harmonic concepts in our epoch gradually progress from a governed and conditioned state, that is tonality, to a free and unconditioned state, that is atonality, while all that is in between represents merely a timid attempt to approach the beckoning goal, *which can only be pure and genuine atonality.*"

Strangely enough, the composers who did not submit to the atonal lure—and they still constitute the majority—nevertheless were swayed by this doctrine of the atonalists. Although from an aesthetic point of view they naturally rejected the idea that music of rank had to be in the extreme atonal vein, they nevertheless, misled perhaps by the prevailing terminology, accepted tonality and atonality as the only contrasting possibilities of musical formation. The situation, they thought, left no room for any further alternative: tonality stands at one end of the road, atonality at the other—all other states are more or less stages between the two extremes. Yet—and this is the decisive point of that theory—there is only one, single road.

An alluring scheme—however, musical reality is not as simple as this. For atonality, that is, abandonment of and liberation from traditional concepts, was only the one, the negative side of the development. But beside this liberation, something far more vital, something far more radical was in the making: a third concept, as different from tonality as it is from atonality, but no less different from the intermediary states, such as extended tonality, modality, polytonality and the like. Indeed, looking at the musical development of the last half century we realize, as it were in retrospect, that from the very time when tonality began to be loosened and was finally abandoned, *the evolution worked in two opposite directions.* One trend worked away from tonality towards atonality,

[1]That this was the innermost idea and purpose of the twelve-tone technique is uncontradictably proved through numerous remarks and directions of its inventor (notwithstanding that he avoided the *term* atonality)—even though later adherents of the technique, significantly, tried to compromise by allowing tonal features, as 'licences', to slip back into the atonal scheme. (We shall return to this later.)

as indicated above. But another trend, which also left classical tonality behind, tended towards another goal, different from and almost opposite to atonality. No specific name has as yet been introduced for the state towards which this trend pointed. All we can say in trying to give a rough indication of the idea in question (later we shall describe it more concretely) is that it is an endeavour to develop patterns of *new tonalities belonging to a higher cycle,* tonalities of a hitherto undefined nature—although in using these terms, which in the musician's mind are connected with certain specific phenomena, we run the risk initially of being misunderstood. If, moreover, we suggest *pantonality*[1] as a linguistic symbol for this new concept, we do it with some hesitation, for pantonality has appeared sporadically in some treatises as a term, even though used there in a vague, casual way, without any concrete meaning attached to it. In fact, it has sometimes been confused with its outright opposite: 'atonality'.

Nevertheless, pantonality in the specific sense as introduced here seems the only fitting designation, considering the three great categories which are to be presented in the following pages as the successive states of harmonic-structural expression during the last centuries. First *tonality*, in which music was rigidly tied to relationships derived from the natural phenomenon of the overtone series. From here, over extended tonality and related intermediary stages, the evolution moved in two opposite directions: one road leading to *atonality*, which cut these ties and thus, when carried to fulfilment, produced a state of outright non-relationship; the other road aiming at *pantonality*, which on a higher plane and with a new type of compositional formation develops the idea inherent in tonality, and in the wake of which a whole complex of new technical devices will be seen to emerge—indeed, even a new concept of harmony itself.

To describe these stages and, in particular, the twofold, divergent directions which made the music of our age strive towards two contrasting goals, and to suggest how tonality and atonality may finally perhaps be led to a synthesis through the rallying power of pantonality is the purpose of this study.

[1]*Pan* is, of course, the ancient Greek word for 'all' or 'whole'. But there is a meaning of universality, of totality, attached to *pan*, somewhat beyond that of 'all'.

PART ONE

TONALITY

TONALITY

THE purpose of this study, as indicated in the foregoing pages, is an inquiry into a theoretically little explored structural concept for which 'pantonality' has been chosen as the technical term. Yet, it will be unavoidable to trace the hidden origin of the new concept first within the realm of those well-known musical provinces: tonality and atonality. Here the reader is begged to follow our deductions with some patience, even if for a few pages the presentation may seem to repeat long-known facts, and perhaps assume almost a touch of the classroom study. We trust he will soon realize that some seemingly elementary phenomena may appear in a different light, if interpreted with a view towards their changed application in a new musical style.

I

HARMONIC TONALITY

The *term* tonality seems to have been introduced into music by the Belgian composer and musicologist Joseph Fétis around the middle of the nineteenth century. It was meant to signify a musical state, which had for several centuries already been in general use, according to which a musical group is conceived (by the composer as well as the listener) as a unit related to, and so to speak derived from, a central tonal fundament, the tonic. This tonal fundament is understood as one note, or, in a more comprehensive sense, as the full triad-harmony of a note, be it major or minor. In fact, the word tonality was probably chosen merely as a linguistically pleasant abbreviation of tonicality (thus also presaging atonality instead of the tongue-twisting atonicality).

To remember this verbal origin is not without importance. For, because people were tempted to use the simpler expression, the meaning of the term often became in later explanations vague, if not distorted. Tonality, according to such semantic uncertainty, was frequently thought to be rooted in relationship to a tone rather than a tonic, in consequence of which the later term atonality becomes, of course, almost meaningless. In other definitions tonality and atonality were described as denoting the congruence or discongruence of a musical group with an underlying scale—the tonic then simply being the beginning, the end or an important note of the scale, without reference to the gravitational, almost magical attraction by which a true tonic holds a musical utterance together and thus endows it with the quality of a group, with 'form'. All these are more than questions of pure terminology. For owing to the far-reaching role theory plays in the understanding of our art, musical terms direct, clarify and sometimes confuse our conceptions of the musical phenomena and may to a certain extent even influence compositional trends.

To return to tonality, then, as a musical state in which a tonical fundament exerts a certain form-building force, this force can be observed in two directions: vertically and horizontally.

Vertically a note becomes a tonic by combining it with its closer overtones to a chord, a harmony. Classical music[1] used these overtone harmonies almost exclusively, that is triads, chords of the seventh and ninth and their inversions. The picture was however greatly expanded and enriched through innumerable devices, such as suspensions, anticipations, passing notes and alterations of all kinds. Yet all these secondary harmonic constructions, through which the available stock of sound combinations was extended far beyond the standard harmonies, were theoretically conceived and had historically come into practical use only as deviations, as 'exceptions' from the basic, the 'true' harmonies—although these exceptions often became more numerous than the so to speak normal harmonies. Originally these exceptions, these 'harmonies

---

[1]The term classical music is here and in the following pages often used in a summarizing way to denote the music of the classical period proper, plus the romantic and even post-romantic period.

outside the harmonies' had as dissonances (i.e. as combinations outside the overtone series) to be prepared and resolved according to certain rules. In the course of time, however, their constant use made them quite acceptable to the ear, and as preparation and resolution were no longer considered obligatory they frequently became perfectly legitimate harmonic entities in their own right. It cannot be the task of this study to elaborate in detail on this subject which is well known to every trained musician and can easily be retraced in any textbook on harmony.

The *horizontal* working of the tonical phenomena that we call tonality is similarly rooted in the relationship of a note to some of its overtones. If a note (for instance, G) progresses horizontally to another note (C), in relation to which the former is its second overtone, the progression appears to the ear as a very compelling, definite step, as if towards a resolution, an end.[1] This feeling of definitiveness, of resolution, is greatly intensified if we add the respective overtones also *vertically* to the two notes, that is, if the progression takes place not only from note to note but from harmony to harmony; for instance, the triad on G progresses to a triad on C (V—I). The B in the G chord resolves then as the 'leading note' to the neighbouring C. Together with the powerful urge of the fundamental G (the dominant) towards the C (the tonic), the progression assumes the quality of a resolution, of a dissonance moving towards a goal, the consonance. The dissonant quality of the dominant is naturally intensified if we use the chord of the seventh or even the ninth rather than the simple triad.

At this point, the following question may call for consideration: why is it that fifths and thirds appear to the ear as consonances while sevenths are already felt to be dissonances, though in the overtone series they follow immediately after the thirds?

Much has been said and written about this problem, both from an acoustical and from a musical angle (these are not necessarily

---

[1]The first overtone, the octave, being almost identical with the fundamental note, does not have this effect.

9

identical). Viewed from the musical aspect, it seems to this writer that the ear will always be inclined to understand any combination of two or more simultaneously sounding notes as a dissonance, *if there is a more consonant combination in the immediate neighbourhood into which the dissonance can be resolved, so to speak, as a suspension.* Thus, since in the immediate neighbourhood of fifths and thirds there are no stronger consonances to be found, fifths and thirds cannot be resolved and are therefore always felt to be consonances.[1] But the (minor) seventh lies beside the consonant sixth (inversion of the third) and the ear is therefore ready to conceive it, as it were, as a 'wrongly intonated sixth', a suspension, which should be resolved.

Returning to the progression V—I, we see why it has that compelling effect, why it creates tonality and through this also can create 'form' in music. For, in the sense described above, I—V—I is not conceived merely as a succession of single chords, but as a unit, as a minute piece of music. As a piece of music, but not yet as a 'composition', since the unity is not brought about by a combination thought out by the creative mind, but by an inherent acoustic phenomenon of relationship between a note and its overtones. In order to state I—V—I, it was merely necessary to discover this natural phenomenon.

The human, the creative factor enters only when I does not progress to V but to some other melodic-harmonic entity—we may call it *x*—and *then* the compelling effect of the dominant-tonic relationship is used to lead the whole series back to the tonic. I—*x*—V—I (*x* can be a chord or a series of chords) is already the scheme of a real composition, formed by Man. In fact, the scheme I—*x*—V—I symbolizes, though naturally in a very summarizing

---

[1]To be exact: (perfect) fifths can never be resolved. But a third is often resolved into a fourth; namely when this fourth is through the context understood as the inversion of a fifth, as in the progression of the leading note to the tonic. Vice versa, a true fourth, being a dissonance, is resolved into a third as when $1\frac{6}{4}$ moves to the dominant.

The question put to the author whether the above is not contradicted by the fact that under certain circumstances a fifth can be resolved into a sixth, must be dismissed with the statement that a fifth may often progress to a sixth but never be resolved in it. Just as even a third can progress to a second, without anyone feeling such a progression to be a resolution.

way, the harmonic course of any composition from the classical period.[1] This *x,* usually appearing as a progression of chords, as a whole series, constitutes, as it were, the actual 'music' within the scheme, which through the annexed formula V—I, is made into a unit, a group, or even a whole piece.

Now it is particularly important to realize—and this is the reason why the whole matter was here described in such detail— that the only step in the scheme which is a 'natural', an overtone phenomenon, i.e. one which *as such* produces the effect of tonality, is the step V—I, or conversely I—V. All other progressions, that is, all chord series symbolized in the scheme by *x,* are the composer's free invention and do not in themselves express tonality (although through tradition many of them have become in the course of time, formulas, clichés). Thus V—I is not merely the archetype but in fact the *only* progression which has the absolute and tonical quality. But if C progresses for instance to D (C—D —G—C), then C—D, a simple and common step though it is, already represents a free melodic progression. There is no compelling acoustic reason why D rather than any other note should be chosen. *C—D is in a sense already an 'atonal' step*, which only by the subsequent G—C becomes a part of a wider tonal (tonical) unit. Similarly, as indicated above, any other harmony or harmonic group inserted in place of *x* can, when followed by V—I, become part of a tonical whole.

All this does not mean that any harmony inserted as *x* will in closeness of relationship have an effect equal to II. D, especially if harmonized as a minor triad, naturally fits much more smoothly into the tonality of C, than for instance does F-sharp. Also A (VI) is a similarly close harmony, as it differs merely by one note

[1]In this general scheme there is an individual case which deserves special mention: when *x* represents IV, so that the formula reads I—IV—V—I. For I—IV is in itself a (transposed) expression of V—I. Therefore, at the moment that I—IV is sounded, the ear may easily accept it as an end in itself, a dominant resolved to its tonic (I being the dominant, IV the tonic). When however thereafter I—IV is followed by V—I, and thus I is re-established as the true tonic, this creates a still stronger effect and the irresistibility of the restored tonality, indeed tonicality, becomes an almost exciting phenomenon. Accordingly it is only natural that this effect was used to the utmost. In the whole of classical literature IV almost invariably appears in one form or another within that part of the scheme for which *x* stands.

from I. Thus all harmonies rooted in and composed of the notes of the diatonic scale represent a series of harmonies more close, more akin to I than any others. *Accordingly, these harmonies from the diatonic scale are frequently classified as constituting the actual compass of tonality.*[1] However, it is very seldom that one finds in classical literature a piece of music, even one of a simple character, which confines itself to these basic harmonies. For, as hinted above, the harmonic variety and complexity of classical music is chiefly centred on the more or less interesting and elaborate way in which *x* is worked out.

There is one further device, about which a few words must be added. Within the framework of the series of harmonies which are represented by *x*, *secondary* dominant-tonic (and tonic-dominant) relationships can also be brought into being, which nevertheless do not destroy the overall tonicality of the group, if followed by the original V—I. In I—III—VI—V—I, for instance, the progression III—VI is in itself a V—I phenomenon. Yet by being understood as a part of the wider whole, the single chords simultaneously retain their role as III and VI. And the same effect can be obtained, even more effectively, if the notes are not simply harmonized according to the diatonic scheme, but independently: for instance, III (in the key of C) not harmonized as E minor but as a major triad or chord of the seventh. This is noteworthy because E—G-sharp—B is from the academic concept of key doctrine outside the scheme. Yet, as is proved by the whole literature, this chord is quite common in C major.

And going one step farther: not only the notes of the diatonic scale but any of the twelve chromatic notes can be and are widely used in classical literature for similar harmonic concatenations.

---

[1]This also accounts for the fact that frequently in theoretical explanations *scales* are presented as the prime elements from which tonality and the whole complex of melodic and harmonic construction are derived and are to be understood. Scales, however, are not musical realities but theoretical abstractions, and as such are themselves derived from melodies and harmonies, not vice versa. In recent treatises on ancient and primitive folklore (and often on modern music) the tendency has become especially strong to base the technical investigation mainly on underlying scales, from which the whole music of the particular realm in question was supposed to have been developed. As a working hypothesis such methods are sometimes useful. But it is dangerous to take the hypothesis too literally and to forget that scales are derived from music, not music from scales.

They will always appear to the listener as a part of the wider tonical unit, though older textbooks described them invariably as 'extraneous', as 'modulations' outside the basic tonality. Indeed, through these harmonies, which Schenker and Schoenberg called secondary or intermediary dominants or tonics (*Nebendominaten*), the wide harmonic range and variety of classical music was largely brought about.[1]

As was to be expected, these secondary harmonies finally became in the course of time entities in their own right and were no longer necessarily followed by their (secondary) tonics —although through this, the terms secondary dominant and secondary tonic retained more of a symbolic than a practical meaning.

But in view of the later evolution the core of the whole matter is that in this way almost all harmonies could gradually be included in the tonical unit. This means, of course, that the textbook scheme of tonality and key had by then already vanished and become theoretical fiction. Indeed, the increasingly frequent use of such complicated and independent intermediary harmonies brought music, at about the time of Wagner's *Tristan,* to a stage where the borderline of classical tonality was almost surpassed. The 'system' began to tremble and today has practically withered away. Yet one cannot forget the riches, the wonders, unsurpassed in the whole history of music, that were produced within the system during the approximately three centuries of its dominance. Finally, however, even empires crumble, one age is replaced by another.

In brief, we realize that classical tonality was in essence centred on the overtone phenomenon. Therefore, as its tonical effect is rooted in harmony and harmonic progression, we may call this type of tonality *harmonic tonality.*

---

[1]The emphasis on the nature of these harmonies as 'intermediary dominants' within one tonically united whole, rather than as modulations or modulatory deviations, as they were usually classified in previous treatises, is one of Schenker's contributions (see Heinrich Schenker's *Neue musikalische Theorien und Phantasien*). It greatly helped to classify and simplify the harmonic picture of a large body of literature. From a more advanced point of observation however the matter is one of terminology.

However, there are also other types of tonality to be found in music, which are indeed different *types*, not merely expansions of the classical type. These different types to which we may now turn have so far never been described in musical analysis. And with this we approach our actual subject.

II

MELODIC TONALITY

How classical, that is, harmonic, tonality was developed, expanded and even abandoned in certain spheres of modern music, will be described later. But modern music also grew from a development and expansion of another type of tonality—a tonal concept traceable far back in history and which is entirely different from the classical type described in the foregoing pages.

In Ex. 1a (see p. 133) a sample of the various forms of the Chant is given, on which the Jews of Babylon still recite certain Biblical texts. The science of comparative music teaches us that tunes like this may be taken as a fairly accurate example of some types of music which the *ancient* Israelites themselves used in their ritual. This musical realm is also of interest to us, as it is well known that the Gregorian Chant (and through it, indirectly, essential parts of our whole occidental melodic concept) were influenced by the music of the Synagogue. Of course, whether the example quoted is absolutely identical with the ancient melody cannot be fully ascertained, neither as to tempo, dynamics, rhythm (if there was any), nor even as to the exact pitch of the notes. However, since the principle of the phenomenon to which our interest is directed does not depend on these details, we may well use this tune as a basis for our examination, as it represents one of the not too numerous examples of truly old music and provides an illustration of the idea to be demonstrated.

In listening to this melodic shape, what strikes us as a main characteristic of its structure is that its notes are held together by a force which would seem to be very similar to that which we call tonality. The E represents a central melodic point, a kind of tonic, and *the whole line is to be understood as a musical unit mainly through its relationship to this basic note.*

15

However, it is equally clear that this is not the same sort of tonality encountered in classical music. (Today we might be inclined, at least for part of the line, to think of the E as the dominant—though this, too, remains vague.) At any rate, the existence of two types of tonality and the difference between them become apparent and can even be demonstrated through a kind of experiment.

The Experiment of Twofold Tonality

Examining this old melody once more, we notice the fact that we can at any point interrupt the line and still bring it to a reasonable close on the E (see Ex. 1b). (The reader is asked to check this by actually listening to all features here described.) But if one were to apply the same method to a classical melody (see Ex. 1c) a strange result would emerge. In the classical melody we see certain points (marked x) from which closing to the tonic (F) is almost inevitable, others (marked ⊙) from which it is possible yet not obligatory, but still others (marked o) from which it is impossible, that is, illogical, unless we want to destroy the innermost sense of the whole line.

The reason for this phenomenon, readily understandable to every musician, is that the second melody is from its very root built as a unit of a strict harmonic-rhythmic pattern. Wherever a closing to the tonic would counteract this idea, a close would be senseless. The first melody, on the other hand, does not show such rigid construction. Here the only tie consists in the fact that the line, notwithstanding its persuasive grouping, is in essence composed as a *melodic* unit that maintains a continuous relationship to the E, to which it always points. As long as this relationship remains alive in one's ear, the line may even be varied and expanded at will without abandoning its tonical quality.

Thus we realize that there are at least two types of tonality (tonicality) in music. One is based on the harmonic and rhythmical structure of the group in question. We called this tonality *harmonic tonality*. It is the familiar tonality of classical music.

16

But there is also the other type just described, that is manifested through melody only. We shall henceforth refer to this type as *melodic tonality*.[1]

The existence of two different types of tonality, if true, would seem to be a fact of such significance that it could change some aspects of our musical outlook, not only regarding past periods but perhaps no less regarding the present evolution. Therefore, to the attempt we have just made to prove the phenomenon empirically by experiment, we may now add some historical observations.

First, there is the fact that became so puzzlingly clear a century or so ago, when Europe began to turn her attention to those various kinds of oriental and 'exotic' melodies of which the Biblical tune quoted above is only one small example—the fact that these melodies not only do not need a harmonic accompaniment *but actually resist harmonization*. When musicians thought that by endowing these melodies with 'nice' harmonies they would sound all the more persuasive to the European listener, their attempts invariably proved to be failures. In fact, it was often technically impossible to force these melodies into the strait jacket of the then current harmonies without changing notes and phrases, in the process of which their whole nature was falsified and their flavour and beauty evaporated.

In addition to this, and complementing it, a glance at music history teaches us that melodies of the other, the 'harmonic' type of tonality could in no way become a considerable part of the general musical production until the harmonic concept (rather than the contrapuntal) had become dominant in music. This is the very reason why we called this type harmonic tonality.

Thus if between two types of melodies, which both revolve around a tonical centre, the one resists harmonization, while the other came into wider use only with the introduction of harmony,

---

[1]The author is well aware that from a strictly musicological point of view it would be necessary to examine many more examples like the one quoted, before something definite about the nature of this type of tonality could be said. However, since the purpose of this study is not a scientific inquiry into old folklore, the one example may suffice to demonstrate *the fact* of a tonical phenomenon that is so different from its classical parallel.

this would seem to be a clear proof of the existence of two different kinds of tonality. And it is only logical that the tunes of the 'melodic' type vanished from the picture the moment harmonic tonality became the dominant concept in music and *that they could not reappear until harmonic tonality was abandoned.* This abandonment took place only towards the end of the last century, that is, with the advent of modern music. It is therefore natural that then also the idea of melodic tonality re-emerged. How this actually happened and in what way shapes of the melodic type of tonality were finally integrated into the rich harmonic and polyphonic design of our musical era will be shown in the following pages.

III

THE TONALITY OF DEBUSSY

A point which must be realized with regard to the foregoing explanations is that the example quoted from the Biblical Chant does not by any means represent an isolated, exceptional case. Rather a majority of old tunes, and not only Jewish tunes, were shaped according to this same concept of tonality so different from the later classical type. However, at the same time it should be understood that not all old tunes were shaped according to this principle. Every once in a while there emerge in old folklore, and especially in early popular European music, tunes pointing to a kind of modern major or minor key, with a clear intimation of a dominant and a leading note. Musicology, although referring to these facts, has unfortunately never gone thoroughly into that whole complex of problems. Confining itself in great part to an inquiry on scales, it has never examined in sufficient detail all the implications of tonality in old music. And by 'tonality' we mean here that quasi-magnetic force through which a musical line is held together and made into a group by relationships between its single parts, which may revolve around each other or around some tonical centre. Such an examination would probably disclose various types of tonality, even beyond the two types indicated in our previous deductions.[1]

This whole question is of all the more interest today, as the Gregorian Chant (itself the source from which our own occidental music sprang) grew mainly from those old oriental tunes and perhaps their Mediterranean derivatives. With regard to the Gregorian Chant itself, it should also be more thoroughly in-

[1] Naturally, there have been quite a few inquiries made about tonality in old folklore (for instance by Curt Sachs and others), but they invariably deal with 'tonality' as a phenomenon resulting solely from tonic-dominant relationships, without taking into consideration the existence of several types of tonality, that is, tonality as described above as a 'gravitational' form-building force.

19

vestigated whether—and if so, in which sense and manner—some of its focal notes, such as the beginnings, endings, and other melodic resting points of the recitative, represent tonics in an inner, phenomenological sense of the term or merely corner notes which traditional practice and theory had developed. If some of them actually are tonics, they must to a great extent be regarded as expressing a kind of *melodic* tonality. For most of the Gregorian tunes, though homophonic, show clearly that the idea of the dominant-tonic effect was, even latently, alien to their nature.

However this may be, when around the turn of the millennium polyphony was introduced, enriching the Gregorian lines, it was natural and inevitable that the first sound combinations were those of the overtone series (fifths or, if sung in inversion, fourths and later[1] thirds and sixths). This means that *harmonic tonality was, at least vertically, now introduced into music.* Horizontally, however, the dominant-tonic effect was still either not yet discovered or intentionally avoided,[2] and the lines continued for a long time to adhere to the character of the Gregorian Chant, that is, to melodic tonicality (if tonicality at all). Only much later was the effect of the dominant, the leading note and the whole harmonic state related to it, developed. This development, as indicated previously, was, and could not but be, coincidental with the rise of the concept of harmony as an autonomous phenomenon, while before that rise, chords were more or less understood as the result of lines sounding simultaneously. At any rate, at the time of Couperin, Buxtehude and Bach, harmonic tonality was already in full bloom and was even theoretically confirmed by Rameau. From then on it reigned uncontested for almost three centuries, so much so that during that period composers as well as theoreticians frequently regarded it as the only natural, indeed, as

[1]'Later' refers only to art music, for singing in parallel thirds seems to have been an established custom in old northern folklore.

[2]But there is the significant document *Sumer is icumen in* from the thirteenth century which seems to point clearly to the dominant-tonic concept. However, this and other problems connected with the first centuries of polyphony have not been, and perhaps never will be, fully clarified. (cf. Dom Anselm Hughes' elucidating chapter 'The Birth of Polyphony' in the *New Oxford History of Music*, vol. II.)

the eternal basis of compositional formation. When it finally became so over-exploited that the musician's mind and ear irresistibly reached for something new, this development took very different shape in two different orbits, the French and the German.

In Germany Wagner's *Tristan* was given to the musical world. Whatever one's aesthetic attitude towards Wagner may be, the prophetic quality of his harmonic structure, particularly as realized in *Tristan,* cannot be questioned. Indeed, his harmonic vision reaches farther into the future than that of his immediate successors. Here for the first time the enduring validity of the old harmonic 'system' was not only challenged but, what in art is so much more effective, creatively disproved. Wagner's successors contributed further to the change which Wagner had so effectively initiated. For instance, Strauss' *Elektra* and *Salome,* as well as some parts of his Symphonic Poems, represent perfect examples of a new tonal state, which might properly be called *expanded tonality.* When this music was first heard it was considered revolutionary, indeed destructive. The professionals viewed it as a departure from all laws of harmony and form, as a complete break with the musical past. Today we realize that its overall harmonic and architectural picture—one is conditioned by the other—is still firmly based on the classical cadence, that is, on harmonic tonality, even though the detail of its texture is laden with series of passing chords, harmonic deviations and free key relationships between the single groups. Yet, as indicated before, in its deeper harmonic essence *Tristan* often seems newer than Strauss' or Mahler's music. Nevertheless, the departure from the classical system had at that time already progressed a long way and when, a few years later, Arnold Schoenberg tried to proceed still farther in the same direction, there seemed to be only one thing left—the very thing which he actually did—namely, to abandon tonality entirely and to assay patterns of music without any tonical relationship, that is, atonality. About this more will be said later. For the present we may turn to quite a different musical world.

For while all this was happening in Germany, another development was taking shape on the opposite side of the Rhine, a development which also departed from and finally gave up classical tonality, but which was centred on a quite different principle. The French development was almost entirely the work of one man, of Claude Debussy.

Debussy chose to replace classical tonality with something that would do away with the harmonic limitations of the preceding period yet retain the spirit of tonality as a form-building force. And to this end he did no less than to introduce, to re-introduce, melodic tonality into music.

Debussy, as a young man, spent some time in Russia, and it is known that some music by Moussorgsky with which he became acquainted made a great impression on him. The most characteristic parts of Moussorgsky's music are flavoured with old Russian folklore and thus, like almost all old folk music, are conceived in some form of melodic tonality. Returning to France and starting his own compositional career, Debussy felt his musical ideal in strong opposition to the German tradition which then dominated the musical world. He is said to have listened eagerly to old French and perhaps Spanish and Basque folk tunes, though the question of his concrete sources and of a possible connection of his own music with them has not really been clarified. However this may be, the melodies with which he adorned his miraculous, new compositions were very different from those of the German sphere. A melody by Beethoven, Brahms or Wagner may often be enlivened by chromaticism, modulatory deviations and passing notes of all kinds. But its kernel, its inner contour as it were, is still invariably conceived according to a latent idea of a harmonic cadence. But Debussy's melodies are not centred on the concept of the classical cadence, on the dominant-tonic effect with its leading note. Yet—and this is the core of this most interesting phenomenon—*there are always tonics sounding through*, that is, focal points on which the melodic shape hinges. If we try to find the secret of this effect we come to realize that these are tonics of the melodic, not of the harmonic type.

Before going into this problem further, we may return for a moment to our previous example illustrating melodic tonality, the Biblical tune. We recognized as its main tonal characteristic the fact that one could reasonably bring the melody to a conclusion on the tonic from any point of its course, without the help of any dominant or any other overtone element, simply through its own innate melodic impulse. But the possibilities for shaping musical entities go even further in this realm. As the reader may easily find out by paraphrasing the tune, any note of the tune can be made to become a new tonic, merely by accentuating it, dwelling on it, that is, by an appropriate phrasing. Indeed, the flexibility of this melodic type is so strong that finally even a deviation from the original line to any other resting point, even if somewhat outside the melodic idea of the original shape, will endow the new note with the quality of a (definite or transitory) tonic, if only it is properly emphasized through the accents inherent in the phrasing.

This is precisely the method according to which Debussy forms his melodic lines. In a somewhat summarizing way one could say: *melodic tonality plus modulation is modern tonality*—at least in the sense which Debussy initiated and which a great part of his French, Spanish and also English successors continued and developed.

This will be demonstrated more concretely in a few moments. However, to understand Debussy's full achievement in this sphere, one must not forget that his compositions are not merely successions of homophonic melodies, as were (at least as far as our knowledge goes) those old folk tunes, but that his basic melodic shapes sound within a complicated web of passages, contrapuntal garlands and harmonies of various types. Yet to grasp the deeper idea of these Debussyan sound combinations we must consider the technical qualities of his melodic patterns in some detail.

In Ex. 2 (see p. 134) a melodic outline of a part of Debussy's piano piece *Reflets dans l'eau* is given—a composition about which Debussy wrote in a letter to Durand that he was shaping it "according to the most recent discoveries of harmonic chemistry".[1]

The shape in Ex. 2a, rising from A-flat in the bass to A-flat—G-flat on top, finally concluding on E-flat, already appears to point to that tonal principle which we subsumed under the term of melodic tonality. Its melodic line is not conceived according to the cadencing spirit which characterizes the classical melody,[2] though, to be sure, its structural pattern is a little different from that of the old Biblical tune, which simply revolved around one note, E. But by sustaining the A-flat as a constant pedal, a relationship of tonical unity, similar to that of the old tune, is alive in Debussy's melody too—a state which is even intensified by the conclusion on E-flat which blends with the low A-flat almost like a unison.

The following group, Ex. 2b, partly imitates the first at a higher pitch. Here the line begins and concludes with C, which similarly blends with the still sustained A-flat. The last figure in this group is repeated and finally falls to D-flat in the bass (bar 35) where the recapitulation starts. Here a particularly interesting feature becomes apparent. D-flat is the overall tonic of *Reflets dans l'eau*. Thus in the traditional terminology the preceding, almost endlessly long pedal on A-flat, would simply be considered as the dominant cadencing into the tonic, just as in any classical piece. However, the upper melodic lines which are contrapuntally superimposed on the A-flat pedal, by no means generate harmonies characteristic of a dominant. These melodic lines in essence are units in their own right, with their own tonical impulses to which, of course, the constantly sustained A-flat pedal adds an increased feeling of oneness.

This concept of a different tonality is still more obvious in the later, corresponding groups of the recapitulation. Here no pedal underlies the design, rather the bass progresses freely, until much later it returns again over A-flat to D-flat. In the traditional

---

[1] Referred to in E. Robert Schmitz, *The Piano Works of Claude Debussy*, Duell, Sloan and Pearce, New York.

[2] Of course, in a forced, artificial manner the line could perhaps also be described in classical (harmonic) terms. See below, p. 26.

terminology one would perhaps, here again, say that the harmonies in Ex. 2c and Ex. 2d are normal secondary dominants through which the line moves towards the basic dominant and tonic. But again the melodic shapes superimposed on these harmonies are melodic figurations on their own, not at all outgrowths (in an overtone sense) from the bass. The groups (2c and 2d) are in their first parts indeed very similar in tonal construction to the Biblical example. Ex. 2c hinges on F, 2d on F-sharp, both however ending with a 'melodic modulation', 2c swerving into F-sharp, 2d into G. When these new melodic tonics F-sharp and G are reached, Debussy harmonizes them in an overtone sense (F-sharp becoming part of the chord of the seventh on B, G becoming part of the triad on E-flat). But this is only a classification from the traditional angle, a classification as it were in retrospect, while the lines themselves are not conceived cadentially. Here it is essential to look at Debussy's score and to examine the full course of the bass within the piece, of which our example (2e) gives but an indication. The bass of *Reflets dans l'eau* (if this dispersed line can at all be called a bass), after the D-flat in the beginning, progresses from bar 16 on as follows: D-flat—C—F; F—G-sharp—B—D (repeated); F—F-flat—E-flat—D; whereupon begins that lengthy A-flat pedal mentioned above, from which the line in bar 35 really concludes in the tonic. All this is certainly not a progression over dominants of any kind, but a freely shaped melodic course returning to its point of departure.

The corresponding section in the recapitulation (bar 48 a.ff.) progresses over B—A—G-sharp to a lengthy E-flat (bar 56) and from there over A-flat to D-flat (bars 62–63). Yet, also in this context, one would hardly venture to classify, for instance, E-flat as the supertonic, A-flat as the dominant and D-flat as the tonic, though theoretically one may be inclined to do so. Only when the line then moves over A—C—A to A-flat (bar 65 a.ff.) does the A-flat finally assume the character of a dominant falling into the tonic D-flat. Thus the entire bass line, looked at for its own sake, is again a shape conceived in the spirit of melodic (not harmonic) tonality, especially since the way in which the bass notes are harmonized—and the reader should study this in the full score—makes it impossible to view them as cadential progressions.

Here we come across a most significant and almost unexpected fact. Whenever the line after its melodic excursions into extraneous regions returns over A-flat to D-flat, although this A-flat may through its different harmonization be far from representing an actual dominant, there will still emerge in the listener's ear, which is conditioned to the musical atmosphere of the classics, a faint feeling that the A-flat—D-flat, even if differently harmonized, is the overtone returning to its tonic. *Debussy obviously uses the pitches of the dominant-tonic progression, rather than their harmonic idea, as a structural device.* Indeed, trained as he was in the classical tradition, Debussy still imbues shapes conceived in melodic tonality with a touch of the old overtone phenomenon. *This blending of two different tonal worlds is one of the most ingenious achievements determining his style.* For it must be understood that the example quoted by no means represents a rare case, an exception as it were, but constitutes a frequent method of his structural formation.

In fact, even the lines which were described above (see p. 24) as samples of melodic tonality can with some effort be classified in traditional terms; for instance the shape quoted in Ex. 2a would thus appear as a kind of suspension—a suspension formed by the whole melodic line—finally resolving into the A-flat harmony. Yet such a formulation would seem rather forced and would not alter the quality of the line which was conceived in the spirit of melodic tonality.

Having thus examined some general principles of the compositional technique through which Debussy established a new concept of tonality in European music, we may still point to some other features, in order to fill in the picture.

1. There is an almost inconspicuous device which nevertheless seems highly characteristic of his style: namely, the frequent use

of lengthy *pedal points*—not merely bass pedals in the actual sense of the term, but sustained 'pedals' in any voice. Seen from the classical point of view these pedal points, as Debussy handles them, often without any harmonic progression taking place above them, might appear merely as a means of escape, designed to avoid rather than to emphasize any clear harmonization of the melodies they support. And indeed this is precisely why Debussy employs them. For they help to let the melodies be understood in their own melodic right and not as melodically extended harmonic progressions, as in a sense are classical melodies.

2.   To make one forget the occasional absence of harmony is also part of the function of the well-known glittering *passages* in Debussy's music. This web of passages and figurations, so much favoured by the composer, was one of the main features owing to which aestheticians of his day affixed the label of impressionism to his music—a term of which he himself somewhat disapproved. The deeper stylistic sense of these passages which in their most effective and characteristic form resist harmonic classification—in contrast to the majority of classical figurative passages—was, again, to circumvent harmonic rigidity. Debussy's passages are in essence melodies, melodies uttered in a swirling flash of polyphonic colour, added to the basically simple course of his compositions.

3.   This retreat from over-emphasis on harmony permeates even his method of harmonization itself. In this respect his frequent use of successions of *parallel chords,* be they chords of the fifth and octave or fifth and ninth, is particularly characteristic. One often reads that he used these chords in rebellion against the rule of parallel fifths in classical music. This is rather a childish explanation, which entirely misses the deeper idea of the ingenious device. Debussy introduced these 'harmonies' because they *are in essence not harmonies at all, but rather 'chordal melodies', enriched unisons.* This applying of harmonic gestures without harmonic content endowed his lines with a 'beauty of emptiness'—an effect which,

however, in works of later, less able composers often became shallow through constant misuse.[1]

4. These chords of the fifth and ninth are also significant from a wider point of view. For they are the first samples of a harmonic concept which later played such an important part in modern musical theory and practice—namely, the concept of *bitonality*. Since melodic tonality, in contrast to classical tonality, is not centred on clear-cut harmonic progressions, it was quite natural that under its aegis chords could emerge, the designation of which was not clearly determinable. In this sense, Debussy introduced those bitonal chords which convey the feeling that two overtone series, for instance two triads, are combined in one harmony. It was the beginning of a way of harmonic thinking from which the whole trend of mixed harmonies evolved and which afterwards led to all kinds of multiple tonalities and finally even to an attempt at a synthesis of all of them.[2]

5. *Use of the whole-tone scale.* This is a feature which usually is mentioned first when Debussy's musical style is described. However, the matter often seems rather misformulated. These little whole-tone phrases—complete scales emerge comparatively seldom—admittedly often appear in Debussy's texture. The reason, however, is not Debussy's search for a new scale system

[1]Once one understands the deeper sense of Debussy's parallel fifths, one cannot fail to refute the amateurish misuse to which the device is sometimes put in the works of would-be modern composers. To interpret a melodic line harmonically in parallel chords is legitimate and may be effective, *if one wishes, as it were, to avoid harmonization*. But to use these chords at random within an environment of organically connected harmonies is a substitute, just as poor and repulsive in the modern as in the classical style.

[2]Though Debussy seems to have been the first to introduce these harmonies as a regular feature, the root of the idea is already seen in some instances of Beethoven's extraordinary manner of harmonization. The clash of the horns with the strings in the first movement of Beethoven's 'Eroica' Symphony, four measures before the recapitulation, was long regarded as due to an error on Beethoven's or his copyist's part. Yet similar harmonies combining the chords of the tonic and dominant, and by the way in the same key of E-flat major, are heard towards the end of the first movement of the Piano Sonata, op.81a (*Les Adieux*). And a particularly interesting example of Beethovenian multitonality is found in his Piano Sonata, op.31, No.2. Here the phenomenon which appears in the development section is centred on the manner of pedalling given in Beethoven's autograph. An alleged error, which some commentators aver is definitely disproved by the repetition of the same markings a few bars later. Artur Schnabel, by the way, in his edition of Beethoven's sonatas strongly upholds the autograph.

but rather his desire to deviate from the regular path of the major and minor modes and their inherent dominant-tonic tonality which did not conform with his musical feeling. Thus in his music whole-tone phrases often come to life beside various other deviations. In general, as was emphasized earlier, composers do not form melodies according to a scale pattern but scales are theoretical abstractions from melodies.

6. As a last feature which must appear characteristic of Debussy's style a certain type of *modulation* should be mentioned. Frequently when Debussy wishes to shift from one tonical orbit to another, he does so without any harmonic bridge, without even any linking chord or phrase, simply by dwelling on a certain note and increasing its accent, exactly in the manner described above in connection with the Biblical tune. A persuasive example of such a modulation, which can be duplicated in numerous others, is given in the quotation from *La Cathédrale engloutie* (Ex. 2f).

All the devices just described add up to the one decisive fact—that Debussy abandoned the rule of classical tonality as the governing principle of harmonic formation; but—and this is the cardinal point—he did not at the same time abandon tonality, that is, tonical relationship, tonical feeling as such. Wherever his compositional lines swerve to unusual melodic concatenations one still feels an aim, a direction towards a goal, towards a resting point. We termed this kind of tonality melodic tonality, since it seems to have originated in the homophonic melodies of old folklore. However, the great, the full structural achievement of Debussy, it should be remembered, must be seen in his combining this new concept with many of the basic ideas of musical construction which he inherited and drew from the works of his classical predecessors—though under his pen even these classical devices often assume quite different meanings. The frequent dominants, for instance, which emerge in the midst or towards the end of his compositions—these good old dominants—appear in their new tonal environment often as particularly charming, indeed surprisingly new harmonic effects. Thus Debussy not only enriched the language of music by inventing *new melodies as a result of his search for new harmonies and a new tonality, but also vice versa, by creating new harmonies from a new melodic impulse.*

Debussy, of course, was not the first composer, not even the first French composer, to try to change the classical harmonic picture. But he was the first to replace the old state by a new positive concept which influenced the evolution. Shortly before Debussy, Eric Satie, though slightly younger, blazed the trail in abandoning or in some cases even destroying, the rule of classical tonality. Satie's influence on Debussy in this respect is historically documented.

The question of Satie's creative significance, which some affirm enthusiastically while others deny it just as strongly, is not under discussion here. This question would depend on more than merely his contribution in the realm of tonality. But with regard to the other question, to whom credit must be given for having initiated a new structural principle of far-reaching consequences in modern music, Satie cannot be considered as Debussy's actual predecessor. The development of the new state of tonality described above, was Debussy's autonomous achievement. Satie, by introducing free and sometimes discordant harmonic progressions was (perhaps simultaneously with that fascinating yet tragic figure, Scriabin) one of the pioneers of modern music. He weakened the old chains as it were, but did not introduce a positive new concept. Debussy, on the other hand, built a new positive concept of tonality in music. This new concept became one of the strongest impulses in the decades after him and influenced a great part of the later French, English, Spanish and American music. Through its further development, enrichment and intensification, and through a blending with many features derived from a quite different musical realm, about which we shall speak presently, a third tonal state came to life, which will be described in a later chapter as 'pantonality'.

PART TWO

ATONALITY

ATONALITY

I

SCHOENBERG'S SEARCH FOR A NEW STYLE

WHILE Debussy was still at work, developing his ideas, a slightly younger, Viennese composer searched in a different direction for a new musical style. The name of this young composer was Arnold Schoenberg.

It is an interesting fact that Schoenberg's creative output was at that time, that is, in his first compositional period, more firmly rooted in traditional, indeed, conservative concepts than was that of his German predecessors, Strauss, Reger or Mahler. A propensity for almost Wagnerian romanticism, of a slightly Viennese variety (perhaps derived from Bruckner), speaks from many parts of Schoenberg's early works, such as his string sextet *Transfigured Night*, the symphonic poem *Pelléas and Mélisande*, his First String Quartet and the cantata *Gurrelieder*. One has the feeling that in these works he clings more carefully, more rigidly, to the classical cadential concept than did his immediate forerunners.

Although, therefore, as far as the music he was writing at that time is concerned, Schoenberg must be considered a traditionalist, nevertheless an impulse, a longing for an untraditional style must already have been deep in his heart. This is proved by the works that followed afterwards, in which the outspokenly traditional idiom was superseded by clear, almost outright atonality.

The change came with surprising suddenness. This is a highly interesting fact to observe. Though Schoenberg at the end of his first period must have felt that he was about to give up tonality, it is astounding that a stylistic bridge, a gradual, organic expansion and loosening of tonality, as we see it in the works of Reger and Strauss, is almost missing in his music. He obviously shunned any intermediary state and, instead, turned from outright tonality to outright atonality. Even in the few compositions, as for instance

33

the Second String Quartet and the Chamber Symphony [1st], where some parts already seem to approach the atonal idiom, other parts are still almost decidedly tonal.

Some observers thought that he had at that time simply not yet found the technical expression for a style which would have helped him to overcome the limitation of the classical harmonic concept *gradually* rather than in a single leap. However this may have been, if it was a deficiency, it was certainly a fortunate one from a historical point of view. Often in the history of the arts technical deficiencies in one sphere proved to be conducive in introducing another technique and thus creating a new style. At any rate, Schoenberg decided to throw off the shackles of the classical concept in one sweep, by force as it were, and in 1909 he published his Three Pieces for Piano, op.11. *Atonality had made its appearance in music.* The effect on the musical world at that time can today, when all this is taken for granted (no matter whether one likes or dislikes the music itself), hardly be imagined by the younger generation. In Vienna, where Schoenberg lived and where owing to her musical past the classical tradition was much more deeply entrenched than in France or England, many concealed their shock by trying to dismiss the whole thing as a joke. Schoenberg, however, soon proved through his next compositions, among which were the *George Lieder*, the Five Pieces for Orchestra, op.16, *Pierrot lunaire* and others, that he was very much in earnest.[1]

---

[1]It should be understood that our presentation, in setting Debussy and Schoenberg in opposition, describes merely the principles and consequently the extremes of the evolution. But there are also in the German orbit, even from the time that Schoenberg developed his style, quite a few examples to be found which leave the established tonal patterns far behind and still point to something quite opposite to atonality. A small yet characteristic sample of this forward-pointing style is quoted in Ex. 3 (see p. 136) taken from Egon Wellesz' opera *Alkestis,* composed in 1923.

In general, the development towards atonality, even the most extreme type of atonality, required much less structural readjustment and structural invention than the development towards those new and higher patterns of multitonality that will be described later in this study. Once the decision to abandon the old systems of tonality and key was accepted, it was comparatively easy to introduce such 'audacious' and 'radical' harmonic combinations as we encounter in Schoenberg's atonal, pre-twelve-tone compositions or in Strawinsky's works from the same period, such as the *Sacre du Printemps* and others. Yet this systemless radicalism did not satisfy the creators: Schoenberg developed his twelve-tone technique and Strawinsky returned to a style much closer to the pre-modern idiom (see pandiatonicism on p. 119).

These works represent the *second period* in Schoenberg's compositional production, before he embarked on his *third period*, which is based on the so-called 'composition with twelve tones'. The harmonic concept which the works of the second period express is, as mentioned above, one of outright atonality or at least a state as close to it as is possible in musical practice. In the Three Pieces for Piano, particularly in the third of these pieces, chords and chordal progressions emerge which reveal little tonical relationship to each other—neither of the type that we call harmonic nor of melodic tonality. Here the musical continuity is maintained merely by thematic consistency and the logical grouping of the phrases: in the first two pieces at times in a homophonic style, that is with a leading melodic line supported by some chordal accompaniment, at other times (and especially in the third piece) in polyphonic elaboration.

If today we survey this period of atonality—atonality pure and simple—in retrospect, some interesting aspects come to light. There can be little doubt that it constitutes in many respects the weakest period of Schoenberg's activity. It comprises not more than ten or twelve works, often of minor size. These works, which, incidentally, are the least frequently performed, are his least interesting ones with the exception of perhaps one or two, as for instance *Pierrot lunaire*. In this work, apart from the fact that a stimulating text recited by the so-called *Sprechstimme* and accompanied by a colourful, half-impressionistic instrumental body keeps the interest alive, there are signs that Schoenberg here attempted an idiom which, had he continued in this direction, would have led not towards direct atonality but to a state more close to a certain new specific style which will be discussed later under pantonality. However, he did not pursue this trend.

But now a most significant event in his development took place: this second period, which began in 1908, ended in a sense in 1912, although the Four Songs with Orchestra, op.22, of 1914, belong in it. The next finished work was published in 1923, the Five Piano Pieces, op.23. In between, Schoenberg devoted himself to other activities, and only sporadically worked on some musical compositions which he never finished. *How is such a lengthy interval of creative silence—an interval of roughly ten years—to be explained?* These ten years of compositional inactivity in a man of Schoenberg's creative energy show that something must have happened in him or in his work, something that impeded the flow of his otherwise irresistible productivity. Indeed, he must have felt that he had arrived at something like a creative impasse and that he had to wait, to search for a way out.

To find the mysterious reasons for this self-imposed lengthy interval of silence we may turn to another part of Schoenberg's creative activities. For there is beside his actual compositional work an authentic source which might help us to see the tendencies, hopes and doubts with which his mind must have been occupied when he entered that decisive period. It is his principal theoretical work, a textbook on harmony, published in 1911.[1]

The effect of this book in furthering Schoenberg's reputation was perhaps more intense and positive than that of many of his contemporaneous compositions, as for instance his piano pieces mentioned above, which had appeared a short while earlier. Whatever one may have felt about the practical usefulness of this treatise as a textbook, at least no one could deny that here for the first time theoretical advice was offered on an artistic level hitherto unheard of in musical instruction. This *Harmonielehre* was not a dry collection of rules but a discourse on the creative impulses which brought the rules into being, and the idiomatic and stylistic conditions under which the rules should be considered valid.

Now, to be sure, the greater part of the book is not concerned with modern music but with the familiar concepts of traditional harmony. Yet, although almost the whole of the book is centred on classical tonality, the reader nevertheless from the beginning is made to understand that what he reads represents merely a

---

[1]The following deductions and quotations refer to and are translated from the original German edition (*Harmonielehre,* Universal Edition, Vienna). An English translation, published fairly recently, is for our purpose of little value, since all parts dealing with aesthetics and questions of principle, which in the original version constitute about half of the book, are omitted.

theoretical abstraction from the musical practice of the past centuries, and that the dawn of a new musical age is fast approaching. Only in the very last pages a few technical indications—not more than indications—as to the nature of the new, 'modern' harmonies are given. These indications of a new harmonic state conform of course with Schoenberg's compositional concept and compositional practice at that particular time in his life, that is, his second, his *atonal* period.

Now by reading Schoenberg's brief description concerning these new harmonies which in his opinion at that time obviously were supposed to form the backbone of his musical language, one cannot fail to be disappointed with the vagueness of his explanations. For here almost every reader would have expected certain enlightening revelations. Now at last one might have hoped to learn something definite, something authentic, about that new unheard-of type of harmonies which at that time shocked the world. Yet no such thing was offered. Apart from a very generalized suggestion that the 'more remote overtones' will henceforth have to be included in the harmonic stock, and a quotation of a few isolated chords from Schoenberg's and his pupils' compositions and those of Schreker and Bartók, no *principle* is set forth, no concrete technical description of the nature of these harmonies is even attempted. Indeed, after his spirited and admirable remarks on the harmonic mechanism of the classical period, the composer seems now, as he tries to advance his own harmonic ideas, to have arrived in his theoretical thinking at an impasse surprisingly similar to that in his compositional production of the same time, which resulted in that ten-year period of silence. That this is not just a presumptuous contention of the present author will soon be proved by calling Schoenberg himself as a witness. But first we must dig deeper into the musical problem itself. What was the reason which at that time prevented Schoenberg from putting to work his full creative resources?

The answer lies in the innermost nature of atonality. For atonality as such is no binding, nor form-building musical force but rather the lack, the negation of such forces. All this will soon be described in more detail. But first, attention should be drawn to another point, namely to a particular concept which Schoenberg developed early in life, and which, although he mentions the whole problem only incidentally and almost casually, nevertheless accompanied his theoretical and compositional work more or less consciously during his whole artistic career. To state this briefly: Schoenberg believed that whether an interval, or for that matter a combination of intervals, a chord, constitutes a consonance or a dissonance, is only a question of habit, of convention, almost of fashion. Thus he concludes that the habit *which for one age endowed the fifth, third and similar intervals with the effect of a consonance could be reversed in another age to a habit which would make these intervals sound as frightful dissonances. Vice versa, those intervals that appeared earlier as dissonances could emerge as smooth, pleasing consonances.*[1]

This idea, constantly pursued by Schoenberg, was later tacitly accepted as a matter of course and retold and reprinted by many of his adherents. Alluring as it may have seemed around the turn of the century when the musical avant-garde searched for a way out from the old restrictive tenets, it can hardly from any sober historical or musical point of view be maintained as a serious thesis.

In general, and quite apart from Schoenberg's theory, there is one thing which makes this whole subject of dissonance difficult to handle; namely, the fact that there is no scale of gradation set up in musical theory for dissonances. The gradation of consonances is quite clear according to the overtone series: unison, octave, fifth, third. But as for the dissonances there is—theoretically—no difference in degree of dissonance between, for instance, an augmented fourth and a major seventh. Both must equally, according to academic rule, be prepared and resolved. And the matter becomes still more complicated if we consider that chords do not consist of one but of several intervals, and in modern music often of a combination of many, even counteracting intervals.

[1]See, for instance, pp. 77 a.ff. in his *Harmonielehre*.

Schoenberg, on his part, did not try to set up such a gradation of dissonances—an endeavour which within the idiom of complicated chords, as in modern music, would probably have been insoluble anyway. Instead, as a justification for the general introduction of more and more dissonances, he suggested that the dissonances represent the 'remote overtones' (in contrast to the close overtones called consonances in traditional theory).

Now it is all too well known that in a physical-acoustical sense the overtone series can be expanded beyond the third, seventh or even ninth. But it is very doubtful whether in a musical sense we hear these further intervals as overtones. Our whole feeling speaks against the assumption that the ear would thus conceive every thinkable note as the representative of a remote, indeed often very remote, overtone; which overtone, besides, would have to be in pitch very different from the note in question and, moreover, would usually have to be lowered many octaves to be identified. From a musical point of view at any rate, this whole theory of 'remote overtones' is unimportant and could at best be considered as an intriguing, if problematical, terminology.

More important is what lies behind it all. Schoenberg confused two different problems. He was entirely right and only expressed the trend of the time in his *aesthetic* claim that further intervals and chord combinations, apart from the customary ones, should be permitted in the harmonic palette. But he was somewhat naïvely wrong in assuming that therefore the musical difference between all these intervals (consonances and dissonances alike) would by the same token be done away with. That the violent, painful and even excessive has as much right to be used in artistic expression as has the gentle and comforting, was a realization that forced itself into the aesthetic and creative evolution around the turn of the century—not in music alone but in all the arts. But that there is no difference between the two contrasting categories and that they can therefore simply be interchanged is indeed paradoxical, if not absurd. The very purpose of including this host of new discords is to intensify and increase the possibilities of contrast, not to obscure or eliminate them.

The truth is that Schoenberg was carried away by theoretical speculation. What he actually was searching for was less a justification for the introduction of more dissonance than *for his new concept of atonality*. For this was the very concept that he tried to express in his compositions of that time. The result was a negative one in both spheres. In his compositional work it enforced on him that ten-year period of silence. As for his simultaneous theoretical thought, one must read what he had to say towards the end of his book, *Harmonielehre*. There, after having quoted the few chordal examples from his own and his pupils' works mentioned previously, chords of the purely atonal type for which no structural explanation is given, he simply declares: "Why this is so and why it is right, I cannot for the time being say in detail. As a whole it may be taken for granted *by those who share my opinion as to the nature of dissonance*."[1] And soon he continues: "Here laws seem to exert themselves. What laws, I do not know. Perhaps I will know in a few years. Perhaps someone else will find them."

He never seems to have known, for he never spoke of this matter again.

To what all this finally amounts is that atonality—straight, unconditional atonality—did not lead Schoenberg to the solution he longed for, neither in his compositional nor in his theoretical search. But here his genius stepped in. For during these years, which must have been a time of crisis for him, he came to the conclusion that in order to proceed further on the road he had chosen, he would have to place atonality on a firm technical basis and develop a method which would bring order into the vague and half-chaotic state to which the unconditional abandonment of tonality had carried him.

The method he introduced was the twelve-tone technique.

Whether even this method brought a solution to the deeper problem which atonality as a compositional principle poses, is a different question which will be discussed later. But certainly it

[1]The italics are those of the present author.

I

This is a facsimile of the beginning and the end of a letter from Josef Matthias Hauer to the author dated February 5, 1924. Next to Schoenberg, Hauer must be regarded as the most important figure among the pioneers to whom the introduction of the twelve-tone idea into music has to be credited. In fact, his first publications to this effect somewhat antedated those of Schoenberg. The gist of the above letter which represents a rather lengthy elaboration (including music examples) on the subject, was to induce the author to turn in his compositions to the twelve-tone method, that is, to Hauer's particular version of it.

enabled him to write those works through which he became one of the most interesting and most discussed musical personalities of our time and through which he exerted an amazing influence on so many composers of our generation.

II

COMPOSITION WITH TWELVE TONES

The *idea* of twelve-tone music was not conceived by Schoenberg. But Schoenberg developed that specific *technique* which the present adherents of this compositional method more or less follow. The differentiation between idea and technique of 'music with twelve tones' should be firmly kept in mind. It is essential for the understanding of our subject throughout the whole remainder of this study. In this sense it should be realized that the thought of abandoning the diatonic scheme and replacing it by one in which the twelve notes of the chromatic scale would have equal rank, seemed at that time a very natural idea. It was, so to speak, in the air.[1]

This writer has much first-hand knowledge of the circumstances surrounding these historical developments. Not only did he have in those days a close personal relationship to Schoenberg,[2] but he was also associated with Josef Hauer, whose works he introduced to the musical world and whose particular role in the whole series of events which accompanied the beginnings of twelve-tone music is well known.

In countless discussions with Hauer the inevitability of placing the new music on a chromatic basis in which all notes would have equal functions and in which no tonic, dominant or leading note

---

[1]R. S. Hill in an elaborate treatise *Schoenberg's Tone Rows and the Tonal System of the Future* (first given as a lecture before The Greater New York Chapter of the American Musicological Society, then reprinted in *Musical Quarterly*, January 1936) surveys some of the early attempts at introducing the twelve-tone concept into music. His paper which, besides containing a still valuable bibliography, gives an exhaustive account of the state in which the whole problem appeared some twenty years ago, is indeed a classic in theoretical literature that no one interested in the subject should fail to read.

[2]The author gave the first performance of Schoenberg's *Drei Klavierstuecke*, op.11 (see Egon Wellesz' biographical study *Arnold Schoenberg*, J. M. Dent & Sons, London, 1925). He also gave the first performance of Schoenberg's *Sechs Kleine Klavierstuecke*, op. 19.

could assume any predominant role was stressed—and this, years before Schoenberg came out with his twelve-tone theory. Hauer from the beginning even emphasized and practised in his compositions the rule, which later became such an important feature in the twelve-tone technique, that within a twelve-tone circle (later called a 'row') no note could be repeated. When soon both Schoenberg and Hauer presented their manifestos regarding the twelve-tone style a more or less concealed rivalry as to the priority of the idea broke out between the two groups.[1]

However all this may have been in detail, one thing which in the light of today's events is decisive cannot be doubted. The twelve-tone idea may have been developed by Schoenberg, Hauer (and others) fairly simultaneously,[2] but the actual twelve-tone technique with its set of rules and devices must be credited solely and exclusively to Schoenberg. And it is this technique which has become such a strong force in contemporary music.

As for the concrete mechanism of the technique it cannot, of course, be the purpose of this study to give any detailed description of its devices. (This may be found in many monographs.) But to a few of the principal features which lie at the base of the technique and to some ideas which emerged from its application, we must now turn our attention.

According to the technique's code every twelve-tone composition is centred on a so-called 'tone row' (*Grundgestalt*). This row is a series of twelve notes built from the notes of the chromatic scale, the order of which is freely chosen by the composer according to his individual intentions in each specific composition. The course of the whole composition or a section of it, then, is formed by a constant reiteration of the row; naturally not a constant literal reiteration, but a reiteration to which certain structural treatments are applied. In the first place, the row can appear either

[1]Schoenberg's system of composition with twelve tones was published for the first time in the Viennese magazine *Der Anbruch* in an article by his pupil Erwin Stein in 1924, while Hauer made his theories known through a series of publications, such as *Vom Wesen des Musikalischen: ein Lehrbuch der Zwölftonmusik*, 1920, and others.

[2]It is highly interesting to note that in some works by the American composer Charles Ives examples of outspoken twelve-tone structures are to be found, composed years before the respective efforts of Schoenberg and Hauer (see Ex. 10a on p. 149).

in a horizontal or in a vertical position or in a combination of both. Secondly, the row can be introduced either directly or in mirror forms (inversion, retrogression, or inversion of retrogression) and also in all transpositions.

These are, in briefest outline, the technical features according to which twelve-tone composition proceeds. But to understand its deeper idea, we must remember the reason why, and the purpose for which, Schoenberg invented the technique. Obviously not entirely satisfied with his pre-twelve-tone style, or at least not convinced of its definitiveness within his creative endeavour, the composer wished to organize atonality on a firmer structural basis. In this respect both points were of equal importance: a firmer technical basis and the achievement of a truly atonal idiom. Of course, some works of his previous period had already been written in a clearly atonal vein, or at least as close to atonality as could be expected in musical practice. Yet to maintain this concept was often a difficult task, and tonal elements again and again threatened to creep into, and to disrupt, the carefully arranged atonal structure. Thus he developed a technique that he thought would make it easier to check tonal inroads and to write strictly atonal music.

Nevertheless, it should be realized that the twelve-tone technique as such, that is, from the point of view of its mechanism, does not exclude tonality entirely. A simple deliberation shows that the twelve-tone row can easily be set up as an almost complete combination of triads. (We shall return to this later.) Still the technique facilitates the attempt to exclude tonality if one so wishes. And this wish, this advice to refrain from any tonal element was strongly emphasized by Schoenberg. Overtone relationships of any kind, be they in the vertical or the horizontal sense, that is, the use of phrases, of chords or chordal progressions that would point to tonical preponderance of any tone within the row, were considered taboo in the twelve-tone technique from the beginning—or perhaps, as we will soon see, particularly in the beginning.

Naturally, Schoenberg well knew that tonality was not only a

harmonic concept but also a structural force of highest importance, as overtone relationships bind the musical utterances, make
them appear as units, and thus create form. Therefore, if he was to
give up this form-building, highly constructive force entirely, he
had, instead, to endow his music with another force of apparently
equal constructive quality. He thought he had found this other
force by integrating into his technique a motivic-thematic permeation of a hitherto unheard-of thoroughness and complete-
ness. *To replace one structural force (tonality) by another (increased
thematic oneness) is indeed the fundamental idea behind the twelve-tone
technique.* Of course, this tendency towards an emphasis on the
thematic phenomenon was alive in Schoenberg from the beginning of his compositional activity—a fact that speaks for the
intensity of his inborn musicianly impulse. This tendency was
increased in his second period, when he abandoned tonality for a
free atonal style. Yet in this second period he must have realized
that the *normal* thematic mechanism was not sufficient to impart
unity to an unqualified atonal style which through the centrifugal
quality of its harmonic design always threatens to dissolve the
compositional fabric. Therefore he replaced simple, unqualified
atonality with *organized atonality* in which he made thematic
consistency—perhaps an exaggerated, overdrawn thematic consistency—the fundamental device in his third, the twelve-tone
period.

This, then, was the picture of the new compositional style: a
highly unified musical fabric in one sense, but with strict avoidance
of any semblance of the other type of unity which is brought
about by tonical relationship.

To understand fully what far-reaching practical consequences
are implied in this idea we may turn to a concrete example. We
choose Schoenberg's Fourth String Quartet, op.37, of which in
Ex. 4 (p. 137) the opening measures are quoted. The constant
recurrence of the twelve-tone row within these measures is indicated by numbers. The example represents one of the typical
patterns in this kind of music. The row sounds first from the
melody in the first violin and spreads vertically down into the

accompanying chords. How did these chords come into being? As the example shows, they must in a sense have been conceived from an impulse to 'fulfil the row'. To this purpose Schoenberg used the following method. He divided the row (the 'melodic row' as expressed in the part of the first violin) into four subsequent parts of three notes each (see footnote on p. 52). The chords in the first six measures are simply vertical formations of the four parts of the row. From the second half of bar 6 on, the *transposed inversion of the row* (starting from G) is played by the second violin, however in an entirely different rhythmical shaping. The first violin 'imitates' the second (again in a rhythmically different shaping), the imitation, however, extending over four notes only, of which the third and fourth notes swerve in contrary motion. At the same time the accompanying chords played by the first violin, the viola and 'cello, express, here too, the successive parts of this transposed row in inversion.

With measure 10 a new group starts. Here the first violin plays *the original row in retrograde*, and also resumes the original rhythm. Again, as in the beginning, the other instruments accompany with chords which are formed from the parts of the row.

Purely structurally speaking, these are patterns of a highly artistic exactitude. However, there are involved in this method certain peculiarities which competent composers, above all Schoenberg himself, solve more efficiently, less competent ones less so. But peculiarities they remain. For once the twelve-tone composer has established the basic design for a group and a few notes of the row still remain unaccounted for, he must resort to the simple but, from a musicianly point of view, rather questionable expedient of dispersing the missing notes *somehow* in the design. We see this procedure recurring invariably throughout the whole of twelve-tone literature. Combined with the postulate that tonical relationships of any kind should be avoided—for the avoidance of such relationships is the core of atonality—the result is that 'harmonies' are created of which the only musicianly justification is the adherence to the row. Here Schoenberg's tenet that the manner in which the ear evaluates harmonic combinations is after all a matter of habit, still lingers on—with all the problematic consequences entailed.

Moreover, while somewhat contradicting the conditions just described, though adding to their negative effect, is a further, and perhaps still more important, problem. Namely, in spite of all efforts of even the most 'orthodox' twelve-tone composer to avoid tonal by-effects, it is almost impossible to set up a series of chord progressions from which no vestige of overtone relationships or implications of them would sporadically sound through. And this refers not only to ordinary triads, chords of the seventh or ninth and their inversions but to all kinds of suspensions, alterations, etc., and often even to mere intervals. In brief, whenever overtone relationships, be they of the vertical or horizontal order, emerge in the otherwise atonal design, the ear cannot help hearing them. For the overtone effect is a natural phenomenon, independent of any style. Since, however, in an atonal design these phenomena emerge not only without but almost against the composer's intention, these hidden relationships will here produce impressions bare of any logic and sense. It is quite a different matter when later twelve-tone composers, consciously and intentionally and against the original twelve-tone spirit, tried to blend tonal and atonal elements, with certain precautions, into one whole. This will be discussed later. Indeed, whether the atonal, the true twelve-tone concept is maintainable at all (a concept which makes no distinction between consonance and dissonance and, in fact, declares the whole phenomenon of harmony non-existent, replacing it by motivic permeation) remains doubtful.[1] *The entire history of the twelve-tone technique during the decades since its introduction seems to point to the contrary.*

[1]Hill's suggestion that the chord patterns of the twelve-tone style themselves may through frequent usage gradually assume an autonomous harmonic meaning and thus provide additional unity to the motivic bond, has not been confirmed by the evolution, tempting as it would seem in analogy to the alterations which have become legitimate harmonies in the tonal realm. The reason is easily understandable. The alterations in classical music, dissonant as they may be, are nevertheless heard as deviations from an underlying design of consonant cadential progressions. But the dissonances (and for that matter even the involuntary consonances) within an atonal fabric are not rooted in such relationship. Their only *raison d'être* is their adherence to the row. And the ear may register this adherence—at least in instances where it is not too difficult to trace—as a meaningful *structural* feature, but will not accept it as a substitute for a *harmonic* quality.

Translation of letter from Arnold Schoenberg to Rudolph Reti (see Plate II).

1/7, 1911

Dear Mr. Reti,

Your analysis has given me great pleasure for two reasons. First, because I gather that the pieces mean something to you. But far more because the acceptance they have found did not remain passive but led you to action. What I mean is that even had your analysis not told me anything new about my piece, still it was, above all, a deed. And a deed is to be valued above all as it springs from a productive urge. But your article says, particularly in the introduction and in the conclusion, very many fine things which really showed me that you are a person who stands very close to my sphere of thought. And this is naturally very valuable to me.

It would give me great pleasure to make your acquaintance. Would you visit me some time? Perhaps you would telephone me one of the next days around two o'clock? But very soon.

Cordial greetings,

Arnold Schoenberg

II

This is a facsimile of a letter from Arnold Schoenberg to the author thanking him for an article which had appeared in the Viennese music magazine, *Der Merker*, June 1911. The article had contained a thematic analysis of the first of Schoenberg's *Drei Klavierstuecke*, op. 11 and was, as far as the author knows, the first analysis ever published on one of Schoenberg's atonal compositions. A translation of the letter appears on page 48.

Twelve-tone Technique in Evolution

Indeed, the history of twelve-tone music consists in great part of the amazing attempt to reverse the technique's innermost idea and nature. And, no less amazing, it is this very process of reversal that has made twelve-tone music such an influential force in the musical evolution of our time.

To explain this paradox it may be recalled that the deeper impulse behind the introduction of the twelve-tone technique was the desire *first*, to create a technical mechanism through which atonality could be expressed in music, and *secondly* (since this abolished the difference between consonance and dissonance), to replace harmonic grouping by intensified thematic structure. It is highly revealing to observe how both these basic tendencies were gradually loosened until in many respects they became almost non-existent.

Astoundingly enough, it was in a sense Schoenberg himself who blazed the trail in this development. Schoenberg in his literary utterances often surprises one with almost visionary recognitions which are in glaring contradiction to his other theoretical deductions and even to his musical practice. Thus, already at the beginning of his twelve-tone activities, he prophesied the change of principle just indicated. In a paper published in 1926 he assures us that "when the twelve-tone system comes of age and the average ear has grown accustomed to it, consonances may safely be reintroduced (while at present certain consonant combinations cannot be used)."

Nevertheless, at that time this idea was merely a prophecy. For in all his specific instructions he warned against letting consonances creep into the twelve-tone fabric. Not only did he emphasize that the reiteration of the same note within the row should

49

be avoided, he even frowned on simple octave doubling. For "to double is to emphasize, and an emphasized tone could be interpreted as a root or even as a tonic; the consequences of such an interpretation must be avoided. Even a slight reminiscence of the former tonal harmony would be disturbing, because it would create false expectations of consequences and continuations. The use of a tonic is deceiving if it is not based on *all* the relationships of tonality."[1]

This strict ban on all features through which even a trace of tonality could re-emerge is one of the basic tenets which the twelve-tone composer was supposed to heed. Yet many of the tonal features (both in a melodic and harmonic sense) which Schoenberg thus wished to exclude, made their unhindered re-entrance straight into the twelve-tone style in the works of his great pupil Alban Berg.

The technical possibility of such re-emergence is not difficult to understand. A simple deliberation tells us that the twelve notes of the chromatic scale can readily be grouped in such a way that the row is formed entirely by a succession of triads or similar chord combinations. Such a procedure would of course not conform with the initial atonal impulse from which the twelve-tone idea originated, but technically it is entirely possible. And Berg in many of his twelve-tone compositions—for instance in his Violin Concerto—did not fail to make use of this possibility. (See Ex. 5 on p. 138, where a technical description of Berg's handling of the twelve-tone idea is included.) In order to avoid any misconception it must, of course, quickly be added that he did not, for all that, deviate from the twelve-tone atmosphere as such. But he never for dogmatic reasons shuns any chordal, melodic or rhythmical shaping which his musicianly instinct urges him to apply. At the same time he preserves the *atonal character, in that he never allows the tonal elements which he includes to determine the compositional course directly.* Through this he produces a mood of pale beauty, of humanized atonality, as it were. It will be indicated later how twelve-tone composers after Berg, developed this

[1]Schoenberg, *Style and Idea*, Philosophical Library, New York, 1950.

trend further, by combining the tonal and atonal elements into one unified musical vernacular.

At present we may turn our attention to another problem which also not only brought a striking change into the twelve-tone concept but even threatened the complete disintegration of its structural idea. The problem is centred in the controversy whether the row is supposed to exert a motival or a non-motival function—a controversy which at times almost split the twelve-tone camp wide open. Yet in the present context not the controversy itself is important, but the fact that in this conflict some of the weakest links inherent in the twelve-tone technique came to the fore.

The motival role of the row would imply that the row has to be perceivable as a musical entity, while if the row were considered as a non-motival element it would of course suffice that the row could somehow be identifiable in the score, even if its single notes were scattered around without much regularity. Schoenberg himself, as could be expected from the initiator of the movement, came out strongly in defence of the motival role,[1] by which means alone the true spirit of the twelve-tone idea could be maintained. This, at least, was his theoretical position. Strangely enough, however, in his musical practice he did not always abide by his own theoretical view. Especially in his later compositional work, many examples can be found where the motival quality of the row has entirely evaporated, leaving it to the analyst's artifices to demonstrate its existence—if indeed, in every instance it was still existent at all. In fact, Schoenberg finally did not hesitate to omit notes in the row or replace them through others in instances where they did not suit his compositional intention. Although from a purist point of view this would appear as a cardinal sin against the spirit of twelve-tonism, it speaks strongly for Schoenberg as a composer. He was much too intense a musician not to follow his musical instinct in a contest between it and his theories.

Today the row can definitely no longer be considered an

[1] In a letter from Schoenberg to Hill, May 1935 (quoted in Hill's article).

element to which a permanent motival role must be attributed—though occasionally it may be. This, at least, seems to be the position which, theoretically and practically, most twelve-tone composers have assumed.[1]

What does all this mean?

It shows that the desire to break through the restrictive boundaries imposed by the technique—for restrictive they were in spite of all assertions to the contrary—became so irresistibly strong among those who practised the technique, that the boundaries were often ignored, even if by so doing the original purpose of twelve-tone composition had to be abandoned. For had the motival role of the row been maintained it would often have become impossible to develop a compositional course of effective variety. Only in the most fortunate circumstances would the composer have been able to produce the compositional design he desired, if at the same time he had constantly to reiterate the literal, the 'genuine' row (even allowing for all the mirror-forms and transpositions). But if the row could be applied merely as a 'functional mode', to use Hill's expression, that is, in a more indirect, vague manner, if it could be dispersed into particles and tampered with at the composer's discretion, then almost any musical picture could be developed through the application of a row to which hardly more than theoretical existence need be ascribed.[2]

Thus the ritual was preserved, perhaps even intensified, but the spirit and inner creed abandoned. And this evolution in the thematic realm was supported by that relaxation in the harmonic-melodic sphere described previously. Atonality was no longer the unalterable theoretical claim of the twelve-tone composer, neither was it his compositional or his aesthetic goal.

---

[1] cf. also Ernst Krenek's study 'New Developments of the Twelve-Tone Technique', *Music Review*, May 1943. Krenek in many of his writings examines various angles of the twelve-tone style. His conclusions are always elucidating, even if sometimes subjective.

[2] In this connexion a further device which had already emerged at an early stage of the technique proved significant: namely, the habit of dividing the row into two or more parts and of applying the mirror-forms and transpositions no longer to the whole row but, whenever it seemed desirable, merely to the single parts, that is, to a series of six, four or three notes—and finally, perhaps, to two notes or even to one. In this way, few ordinary designs of a chromatic character are thinkable that could not be labelled twelve-tone structures.

It is in this sense that reports about recent musical events in Europe should be understood. We hear for instance about twelve-tone symphonies and operas of a 'very loosely knit, entirely free twelve-tone structure'; or that 'if one did not know that Mr. X writes in the twelve-tone technique one might not suspect it from the sound of the music itself'.

Indeed, the freedom from the law to which the twelve-tone composer had allegedly submitted has become a point of emphasis stronger than the law itself. The truth of this becomes most apparent in the explanations by the twelve-tone composers themselves. Their discussions no longer seem to revolve around the problems inherent in the twelve-tone technique as such but rather around the one obviously all-important question: to what degree and in which way can its law be circumvented or outrightly ignored?

Josef Rufer, in his interesting study on the subject,[1] publishes a number of statements by twelve—indeed twelve—of the best known twelve-tone composers. After a solemn bow to the greatness and significance of the technique, each of the dozen takes pains to show how his particular handling of the twelve-tone idea differs from the original system.

Rolf Liebermann, one of the most brilliant of them, has coined the almost classic slogan of the "individual treatment" by which the technique was "indeed transformed by strong individual personalities". "The technique", he adds, "was simply the starting point and basis. . . ." Still more outspoken is Luigi Dallapiccola, whose affiliation with the twelve-tone method is particularly interesting, as he endeavours to instil into its mechanism a touch of Latin melodiousness. Dallapiccola says: "Today, more than ever before, I am trying . . . to explore all the possibilities of the system and to work patiently towards its clarification, by means of sensibility and not of theory. The definite rules of this new language . . . which, like any other language, is a living thing, will only be determined *a posteriori;* they will be codified

[1]Josef Rufer, *Composition with Twelve Notes*, Rockliff, London, 1954, and Macmillan, New York, 1954.

in the future by theoreticians on the basis of what creative artists have actually done in their works." But most unequivocal is the position stated by two other adepts, Matyas Seiber and Richard Hoffmann. Seiber says: ". . . orthodox twelve-note composers and theoreticians will say that this is not 'proper' twelve-note music. That seems to me not of the least importance at the moment; the only thing that interests me is whether I succeeded in writing some real *music.*" While Hoffmann—significantly the youngest of the twelve—even declares: " . . . the inexperienced composer should not emulate the 'sophistic' twelve-note composer, who would have little—if anything at all —to say if his powers of invention were not goaded on by complicated tables of permutations of the series. In fact the over-emphasis on the logic and 'magic powers' which certain faithful adherents of this kind of composition have introduced into it has exceeded all bounds." Certainly, words like these require little comment.

Though these quotations would suffice to demonstrate the general direction towards which the recent twelve-tone evolution tends, two more utterances may be added as they are of particular interest in the light of our later deductions. One is by Humphrey Searle, who also must be credited with the impressive rendering into English of Rufer's complex study. He declares that in his own sonata he wished "to combine Liszt's idea of 'thematic transformation' with Schoenberg's practice. The form is similar to that of Liszt's sonata. . . ." Winfried Zillig, finally, says: "I am coming more and more toward the mysterious and compulsive connexions with tonality . . . "—obviously connexions of his own twelve-tone music with tonality.

No doubt all this points to an undeniable clash between the older and newer concept of twelve-tone music. Yet the nonpartisan observer must be careful not to condemn either side. There must have been strong and genuinely artistic impulses at work which brought twelve-tone music to life and made it such a widespread force in the music of our time. But no less strong, no less genuine must have been the impulses which seem to drive twelve-tone music out of its own shell.

What is the explanation for this astounding process whereby 'composition with twelve tones' not only changes its character but even points to something which is almost opposite to its own nature? Whereby composers who actually do not practise this technique still like to call themselves twelve-tone composers? Perhaps the following pages, though they are directed towards quite different problems, will include some answers to the present questions.

PART THREE

PANTONALITY

PANTONALITY

I

Bitonality and Polytonality

ATONALITY and twelve-tone composition characterize only a specific and fairly small part of the creative output through which the recent musical evolution has manifested itself. A great number of composers did not wish to express themselves in atonal structures but took over and further developed that new concept of tonality which Debussy had initiated. This remark, however, should by no means be interpreted to signify that the composers outside the atonal and twelve-tone camp were simply imitators of Debussy's style and idiom. It is meant merely to imply that they followed, consciously or instinctively, the direction to which Debussy had pointed in his endeavour to change that state of harmonic tonality which had characterized the classical period.

The search for a new musical style was not carried on solely by the two great antipodes, Debussy and Schoenberg. There were a few others who, though their influence did not prove so far-reaching, nevertheless contributed greatly to the evolution. One eminent figure in this respect, already mentioned in our deductions, was Alexander Scriabin. Scriabin's artistic path was somewhat blocked by inner and outer obstacles. His aesthetic vision and the practical realization of his musical ideas were not as balanced, clear and unified as were those of Debussy, nor as definite, bold and revolutionary as Schoenberg's work. Yet Scriabin's influence on both of these composers and on the whole musical world cannot be overlooked. Though his talents were somewhat dissipated, he was still more than a mere experimenter. In some of his most mature works he developed musical structures of real strength and beauty which have not yet been fully exploited. In the present intensified search for the origins of the new musical style Scriabin's music may still experience a revival.

Another kind of pioneer, the humble and venerable Czech composer Leoš Janáček, should not be forgotten in this connexion. As a Moravian schoolteacher somewhat aloof from the larger musical centres of the world, Janáček nevertheless, through several theoretical publications and still more through his inspired and highly individual compositional work, helped to round out the image of modern music which during his lifetime had begun to assume ever wider significance. He was able to instil a human impulse which is not very often encountered in modern music into his harmonically and rhythmically new fabric. Much of his music awaits discovery by wider circles.

As for Debussy, apart from that idea of melodic tonality which he introduced, there is also another, more specific compositional device observable in his music, to which we already referred briefly. It is the use of harmonies brought about by a combination of two or more triads or, more generally, of several overtone complexes. Sporadically such bitonality is already encountered in the works of Strauss and Mahler or, for that matter, of Wagner and Chopin, and can even be traced as far back as Beethoven.[1] But in the music of Debussy it emerges as a regular feature and forms the beginning of a far-reaching development. For in contrast to atonal chords which on the surface may appear more audacious but do not represent true musical organisms, those bitonal or tritonal harmonies include the truly revolutionary and positive element of several simultaneously sounding tonics. And these multiple tonics—first only tonics in the vertical sense—often become in the evolution after Debussy full horizontal tonics, that is, tonics creating tonality, creating form. Thus a state of simultaneous tonalities emerges—tonalities that cross, overlap, complement or even oppose each other (not merely contrapuntally juxtaposed tonalities in the sense of 'polytonality' à la Strawinsky or Milhaud, about which we shall speak presently). For in those bitonal harmonies *the ear instinctively singles out the*

[1]See footnote on p. 28.

tonics, and connects each of them to any successive phrase with which they can enter into a tonically meaningful relationship. This phrase may be found in the same voice or in a different voice. Moreover, the tonality by which the connexion is perceived may be either harmonic or (perhaps even more often) melodic tonality. In this way a musical language may develop, enlivened by diverse tonical sub-groups within one design, without the whole group necessarily resting on a tonical fundament in the classical sense—in fact, often resting on no fundament at all. Accordingly, it is not surprising that in the beginning of the modern development such harmonies were simply labelled atonal, although they are not only *not* atonal but express in their multitonicality almost the opposite principle.

Before elaborating further on this idea we may insert a few remarks on that other type of construction mentioned before, which is usually subsumed under the name of polytonality. The very term polytonality, which, by the way, seems hardly a fitting expression for the rather primitive idea it signifies, was introduced to denote a compositional method where two musical lines which are in different keys appear contrapuntally juxtaposed. The main weakness of the term, therefore, lies in that it conceives tonality as identical with key rather than in its wider aspect as a tonically unified group. The idea emerged in the first stages of modern music, probably from a kind of *épater-les-bourgeois* spirit, although there may also have been some more serious impulse involved. Polytonality was used by Busoni, Strawinsky, Casella, Milhaud and others, mainly when a touch of grotesque humour was intended.[1] None of these composers made polytonality his exclusive or even his regular medium of expression. They applied it merely for certain specific effects. In fact, the whole idea had no continuation in the evolution.

[1]However, Mozart already used polytonality in a composition entitled, significantly, *Ein musikalischer Spass* (A Musical Jest). In fact, a polytonal formation is found as far back as the sixteenth century in a composition by Hans Newsidler (see the *Harvard Dictionary of Music* under 'Polytonality').

II

Fluctuating Harmonies

Approaching the concept of pantonality and thus arriving at the core of our inquiry, we may as a point of departure restate our words on the effect of bitonality: ". . . . in those bitonal harmonies the ear instinctively singles out the tonics, and connects each of them to any successive phrase with which they can enter into a tonally meaningful relationship." In the previous context, however, this description referred merely to a type of compositional formation, which became apparent in those comparatively primitive bitonal or tritonal harmonies found in the Debussy example. Later, however, when multiple harmonies of a more complex nature emerged in modern composition, not only vertical chord combinations but also elaborate horizontal combinations of diverse tonalities were the organic consequence. And these more complicated configurations express a principle distinctly different from that which we previously described as atonal.

As an illustration of what is meant we may turn to Ex. 15a (on p. 159) in which the initial group from one of the author's compositions is quoted.[1] At first glance these bars may look just like any atonal design. On closer examination, however, one easily recognizes that this is a blending of several tonically based ideas—a blending, not a clash of keys as in polytonality. The phrase marked (I) is obviously based on C-sharp; the phrase (II) on A; while the tonical designation of the phrase (III), which later leads to a kind of D minor, is not clear—it may be B or E. Yet it is

[1] With regard to this and a few other examples taken from the author's own compositional work the reader is urged most kindly to avoid the misconception that they were singled out as supposedly representing the most effective embodiment of the phenomena in question. But rather than operate in other living composers' realms as in an analytical laboratory, the author thought it more just in certain instances to use, though reluctantly, a few measures from his own compositions. In any case, to comprehend the full implication of the trend described, the reader will have to search through a considerable body of contemporary literature.

certainly a tonal, not an atonal idea. It is impossible to determine which of these three tonical phrases is the fundamental one (except for the first few measures when phrase (I) sounds alone), especially since harmonic and melodic tonalities are here mixed. Phrase (I) for instance, is only in a harmonic sense based on C-sharp as a tonic, as stated above; but at the same time it supports the little figure D—C—A—G—C, with D as a tonic in the melodic sense. And the question of which tonic is the fundamental one, depends simply on which one the ear singles out as the main pillar at any given moment. In fact, the tonical basis will *fluctuate* throughout the whole group. But it does remain tonical despite the fluctuating quality.

Here a point of fundamental importance should be noted. Though the various phrases just described represent independent tonical lines, they are not placed at random one beneath the other, but blend into one unit. In fact, *they are held together by a kind of consonant relationship*. For instance, in bar 3 the A minor phrase in the lowest part, B-flat—A—C—A, blends consonantly with the phrase D—C—A—G—C above it. Or: the B-natural in the soprano (bars 7 and 8) combines harmonically with the C-sharp and G-sharp under it. Thus the design, though spreading freely in various directions, still does not lose its tonical atmosphere.

In general, because of this over-all tonical atmosphere, the ear will connect any fitting notes or particles to tonical or quasi-tonical units. In this sense the low B-flat in bars 7 and 8, representing remainders from phrase (II), will be connected to the C and A above it, and thus suffice to recall the full thematic meaning of phrase (II). Also when the line developed from phrase (III) concludes in D minor (bar 10), the ear cannot help but relate this D to the D which sounded in the opening chord of the piece and since then continued at the beginning of every bar—in spite of all the various tonalities in between.

The idea here under discussion may become all the clearer if we try to demonstrate it in a comparatively simple, yet beautifully lucid, example. It is taken from the Second Piano Sonata ('Concord') by the American composer Charles Ives. The two groups quoted (Ex. 10b and Ex. 10c on pp. 149 and 150) represent the beginning and the end of the sonata's last movement (Thoreau).

Turning first to Ex. 10c, there can be little doubt that, at least in its first part, the C major harmony forms a kind of tonic. However, we do not hear a pure C major, but a C major under which an organ point on A is heard—and this bitonicality is steadily maintained throughout the whole group. Before the conclusion, then, the A is used to introduce an atonal phrase recalling the opening bars of the movement (as seen in Ex. 10b). The phrase ends on C-sharp (at the *pp* mark), where, with the A and the following G in the bass, it forms a kind of intermediary dominant announcing the D minor chords which enter presently in the higher voices. Yet while all this develops, and in spite of the C-sharp in the soprano, the original tonic on C-natural is still reiterated in the basso continuo. Only finally a G in the bass replaces the C (and A) as a root. Simultaneously another quasi-tonical phrase, a kind of B minor, emerges in the middle voices. This B minor phrase of utter tenderness leads, atonally as it were, to a concluding C-sharp. Yet through all these tonalities (and atonalities) the original tonical basis—C-major with an underlying A—sounds through. The last audible harmony (G—D—C-sharp—A) is simply the dominant of C major with an added atonal C-sharp. But now note the following, through which alone the meaning of the whole design becomes understandable: in a technical and acoustical sense it would be quite logical to let a C major chord follow as a conclusion of the piece (one should try this out on the piano), though admittedly from a musical-artistic point of view it would be a sin even to think of such a 'solution' through which the poetry of the design would be irrevocably destroyed.

On the basis of the foregoing and again considering the structural idea underlying the whole group, we repeat our initial assumption: C major forms, at least before the end, a kind of superior, if latent, tonic *which is expressed in a final cadence:* VI (A), followed by II (D), followed by V (G), followed by—nothing, since the expected concluding C is no longer audible. In addition, and in the midst of all this, however, a B minor harmony and some atonal phrases leading to a most tender, yet profound, conclusion on C-sharp, develop a specific atmosphere of oscillating tonical relationships.

To sum up: in this design no unequivocal tonality actually reigns. For though, viewed from the context of the last group, C seemed to become the over-all tonic, expressed through the 'cadence', a tonical A still introduces the group emphatically in the bass. And this assumes all the more importance, for not only this last movement, but also the first movement, begins with the same A (as one can see from a glance at the score). Thus we have: C and A as over-all tonics, G as the last audible root, furthermore the harmonies of B and D, not forgetting the atonal phrases in between, concluding on C-sharp (which, by the way, in its harmonic context should be understood as D-flat). And all these tonics and harmonies overlap, sounding almost simultaneously, like rays reflected from a set of mirrors—truly this is 'pantonality'.

Thus both the Ives example and the preceding one reveal a tonal state that cannot be readily tabulated, yet which has a clear flavour of *tonality as such*.

To render this provisional picture of the new structural state in question more comprehensible, it should be pointed out that the material from which the groups quoted are formed is in its detail atonal, indeed truly atonal, not merely tonal spiced with discords. Yet this atonal detail is so distributed that the groups as a whole evoke an atmosphere that expresses neither atonality nor tonality but a more complex structural condition, a multitonal (or to expand this term to our own concept) a pantonal state. Here we have reached the nerve centre of our problem. *There are two types of musical lines to be found in music, which at first glance might seem to be of the same order, that is, both seem to be atonal. Yet of these two types, the one is conceived in a spirit of unconditional tonical non-relationship, while the other is conceived in a spirit of, so to speak, indirect tonality—that is, tonality which does not appear on the surface but is created by the ear singling out hidden relationships between various points of a melodic or contrapuntal web.*

Of course, two small quotations can hardly give more than a slight intimation of a new category of structural formation. Yet if the reader will pursue the idea throughout numerous examples from contemporary literature in which similar formations, though technically a thousandfold varied, can be observed, he will realize that here *a new concept of harmony* arises. To clarify this decisive part of our investigation, a few explanations must be inserted in which the specific observations emerging from the examples above may be widened to a more general outlook.

Moving Tonics

'Harmony' as a musical term has usually been attributed to a chord—either an actual chord or an expanded chordal entity. Even when understood in its functional quality within a harmonic progression as a 'degree', and comprehended as an underlying pillar for a whole group, harmony itself has remained, if not a static, at any rate a self-contained conception, either centred on its (audible or implied) fundamental note, as in classical music, or without such a foundation, as is often the case in the modern era. Of course, progression from one harmony to another was always one of the main factors of motion in music. But in the style envisaged here, not only harmonic progression, but harmony itself, often becomes a fluctuating phenomenon, a phenomenon in motion. It is not expressed through a chord, or even a group of chords, but rather through the relationship between various chordal entities, indeed, through a full musical design. In such a design there will always be a number of single notes, chords, or particles of chords, or even wider phrases that will, for smaller or larger stretches, assume the (transitory) role of a tonic. Some tonics may unify only a minute figure but others may reach into subsequent phrases. Suppose, for instance, that in a chordal group a certain note has been understood as a tonic, whereupon a new group enters, and that in relationship to this new group another note of the first group assumes more weight. Then the ear will instinctively accept this second note as a new tonic. In other words: *the tonic within the first group will be shifted, will move as it were, to another note.*

This concept, then, of movable tonics, of fluctuating harmonies, is the point of departure for the understanding of the phenomenon of 'pantonality'. In order, however, to make its nature more clearly visible we may demarcate the principle here involved from other concepts, from which it must be strictly separated if misconceptions are to be avoided.

1. *Tonal centre.* Analysts of modern music from Debussy on have become reluctant to single out harmonic successions but rather try to explain the harmonic design by pointing to certain groups and harmonic pivots as tonal centres. And this terminology, a natural consequence of the new idiom, was often more pertinent than the previous tabulations of single chords. Yet it was somewhat of an over-simplification, since a whole range of important features thus eluded observation. But the term is even less appropriate to signify the new and more complex structural phenomena described in our present deductions. For the fact that tonics focus no longer on a note or a chord but on a whole design, tells only half the story. The second, more significant half is based on the fact that in these centres the tonics themselves fluctuate, indeed, oscillate between different points within a group.

2. *Extended (or expanded) tonality.* Neither should pantonality be understood as merely identical with even a fairly outspoken degree of what is usually referred to as 'extended tonality'. For this latter term characterizes a state where one basic tonality still prevails, in spite of various melodic and harmonic figurations which may have been added. The characteristic attribute of pantonality, on the other hand, through which it becomes a truly new concept and not merely an increased expression of classical tonality, is the phenomenon of 'movable tonics', that is, a structural state in which several tonics exert their gravitational pull simultaneously, counteractingly as it were, regardless of whether any of the various tonics ultimately becomes the concluding one. To keep the two concepts apart is all the more important as in recent investigations the attempt has been made to explain all modern music, even its truly atonal part, more or less as a kind of

camouflaged tonality. The logic behind these attempts was that the analysts felt the force of pantonality emerging everywhere in modern production. Since, however, this force had not yet been defined, they tried to explain any novel structure as a quasi-hidden, sometimes perhaps distorted, tonality. The problem is not a simple one, for it is true that historically speaking 'extended tonality' was the predecessor of pantonality into which it has finally been transformed. And, as in all artistic evolution, there is in practice no strict date and demarcation, where one can say: here extended tonality ends and pantonality begins. Yet to distinguish between the principles of the two is essential.

3. *Undefined tonality*. This concept, which sometimes became apparent in post-classical music, is closely related to extended tonality. Even in the music of Strauss, Mahler, Sibelius and others there are often sections which are decidedly tonal, although their actual key relationship cannot be determined. They float in the realm of several keys without deciding, as it were, upon one concrete tonic. Yet they are very far from that other state to which our present explanations point and in which diverse tonics intertwine and radiate, spreading their influence in all directions.

4. *Tonality*. The demarcation between pantonality and simple tonality was the core of our preceding deductions. Here the one important fact should be recalled that whenever tonics are mentioned throughout our whole presentation, they are invariably meant to include equally tonics of the harmonic and of the melodic type of tonality. That both these different types can now be applied alternately, in addition to the diverse features described above, warrants the extensive compass of the structural possibilities inherent in pantonality.

5. *Atonality*. No less important is a last feature which has already been indicated but which now should be stressed particularly. It is the fact that in the pantonal picture much of the atonal fabric, many of the melodic figurations and chordal combinations of atonality—indeed, of atonality, not of simple chromaticism—

can be and usually are included. Yet the significant point is that the composer still does not use this material to develop an atonal picture in the sense of the original twelve-tone technique, but rather uses the atonal figurations to form those new constructions just described in which a diversity of tonical impulses elevates the atonal shapes to a design of uninterrupted coherence.

Atonal tonality, fluctuating harmonies, movable tonics, tonics of different types—a new compositional category, *pantonality,* is in the making.

III

SPECIFIC FACETS OF PANTONALITY

In the foregoing chapter an attempt was made to give an initial idea of the conditions characterizing the concept we call pantonality. Yet to obtain a clearer picture of the various problems involved it will be necessary to view the subject from several angles.

Consonance and Dissonance

There is first the question of how in the realm of pantonality the problem of consonance and dissonance is treated, that eternal problem about which aestheticians speak so much and say so little.[1]

Off-hand, one might surmise, since pantonality according to our previous description points away from the classical tonal concept, that the distinction between consonance and dissonance

[1] A discussion, on a musicological level, of the consonance-dissonance phenomenon from its origin on would require a study in itself which cannot be attempted here. Two main points, however, which lie at the centre of the problem may be recalled.

First, the fact that the intervals formed by the first three overtones (octave, fifth, third) and their inversions are as consonances separated from all other intervals felt to be dissonances. An explanation of this never fully clarified feature was attempted in a previous chapter (see p. 10).

Secondly, the fact that a gradation of dissonances was never included in the framework of musical theory. Such a gradation was recently attempted but in this author's opinion hardly achieved in Paul Hindemith's elaborate study *Craft of Musical Composition*. The famous composer set himself the task of constructing a musical chart by means of which every thinkable chord combination of any style or time (past, present or future) could be tabulated as to its place and value. But in his endeavour not to lose himself in the infinite—is music, however, not infinite?—he regards every chord, even every simple interval, as an unequivocal phenomenon, the musical meaning of which having been established once and for all by its acoustical properties. However, in music, in contrast to acoustics, intervals and chords have ever-varying, rather than fixed, static meanings. To quote a most elementary example: a fourth which Hindemith classifies as an unequivocal consonance (the 'second best' in his gradation of values) is in practical music a consonance only if the texture within which it appears makes it understood as an inversion of a fifth (through which its upper note becomes the root). All these are long recognized facts of which the composer Hindemith is naturally well aware. Nevertheless, he builds his musical cartography of 'good' and 'bad' intervals and chords on such a problematic evaluation, centring each chord on a rigid, unchangeable root, regardless of its role within the design. Consequently, we find in his theory not the faintest trace of all those complex phenomena around which a great part of modern musical construction revolves: bitonality, crossing tonalities, pantonality—and, for that matter, quite logically not even of atonality, which he somewhat too simply dismisses as a bluff or lack of invention.

would either be abolished altogether (as it was in atonality); or, if the distinction were retained, that the borderline between consonances and dissonances would be shifted to include more intervals in the consonant realm. Yet, logical as these questions may appear, they must be differently formulated if they are to lead to a fruitful conclusion.

As a point of departure, a fact may be recalled which was already mentioned on a previous occasion: namely, that with the beginning of the atonal development the belief in a kind of interchangeability of consonances and dissonances gained popularity. Schoenberg initiated the idea which quickly spread among his adherents. But even many composers who did not actually follow his footsteps, unhesitatingly accepted the theory which seemed so enticing. At the time of the dawn of the modern idiom such a host of new harmonic effects sprang up—effects which then seemed new and exciting but which today often appear tame, if not cheap—that almost every composer considered himself a radical and proudly accepted any new, 'revolutionary' doctrine— at least theoretically. The practical evolution, however, proved otherwise. The reaction of our ears to the fundamental antagonism between consonance and dissonance has not changed one iota. What has changed is merely the aesthetic interest. The modern composer wants to make use of an incomparably larger amount of dissonances than his classical predecessor and also to change the way of their application. And together with the increase of dissonances he further wants to reduce the use of consonances, in fact, to do away with certain consonances, such as triads or the like, almost entirely. But this is the result of a new *aesthetic* approach rather than a new acoustic evaluation. The atonalists say that in an environment of modern harmonies consonances cannot be tolerated since they would here sound just as dissonant as dissonances in the old style. This, of course, is a somewhat inverted way of putting it. Consonances do not sound as dissonances in the atonal idiom but merely as alien, and therefore as stylistically disturbing elements in an otherwise homogeneous fabric.

Here it is important not to forget that dissonances and discords are not identical. Dissonance is a musical, while discord is an acoustical, phenomenon. Dissonance simply points to a state of tension. It can sometimes be a discordant, that is, an offending sound, but just as often have a 'beautiful', a pleasing effect. This whole question depends chiefly on the composer's intention and art of phrasing. Dissonances will not sound discordant if they appear as parts of a tonical construction, even a complex multi-tonal construction; and if the design within which they come into being is based on a truly *thematic* idea, not merely on the accumulation of motivic artifices. The paramount importance of the thematic point will become particularly clear in the remaining examples of our analysis.

Returning to the idea of dissonance, there is no doubt that its nature has not changed. What has changed is merely what the composer wishes to say. This author remembers how some thirty years ago he was told by Alban Berg—and the words still ring in his ears—that in a few decades "our music will sound as natural and simple as Mozart's sounds today". The decades have passed and Berg's music has held its place but his words have not come true. Because his music was from the beginning not meant to be like Mozart's but was intended to reflect the tense excesses and, in fact, morbidity of our age. This difference in intention is in itself not a criterion of a greater or lesser artistic value or, to be perhaps more exact, of a greater or lesser artistic mastery. And as for Berg, he managed—and this points to his greatness—to blend his and his time's tendency towards excess and conflict with an immanent longing for beauty and harmony. In the music of other composers close to him the negative forces were much less challenged.

Coming back to pantonality and its relation to the same problem, it is thus not the number of dissonances that counts but the role which the dissonant harmonies play in the compositional design. In the music of our time, whatever its individual style, there will be long stretches where true consonances hardly appear. Yet there is a basic difference. In the specific atonal sphere the dissonances appear *without being identified as dissonances*—as though there were no tension, no 'longing to be resolved' inherent in them. But in the 'pantonal' musical utterances of our time, which at their face value may appear just as full of dissonance as any tonal design, we see quite a different tendency.

To demonstrate the nature of these different musical atmospheres we may turn to Ex. 6 and Ex. 7 (on pp. 142 and 144) and compare the two compositional pictures, the first example tending towards the pantonal, the second towards the atonal concept.

In Ex. 6 the opening group of the third movement from Béla Bartók's Music for Strings, Percussion and Celesta is quoted. Trying to classify the first harmony in this design, we come across the combination F-sharp—B—F in bar 4 (to which some passing notes from the timpani-glissando should be added). This certainly does not sound like an utterance to which any vestige of tonality could be attributed. However, the B soon turns out to be a suspension which in the following bars is resolved into C, while the F falls to E (bar 6) where the theme starts in the viola. Thus the basic harmony F-sharp—C—E is established, of which F-sharp is unquestionably the root. This is shown transparently by the viola theme which is *melodically* centred on C-sharp rather than on C. The C, though, is continued in the timpani (and supported an octave lower by the double bass), yet it appears in this whole context and through the delicate instrumentation merely as a beautifully dissonant auxiliary note.

The principle through which this structure grew now becomes clear. It is based on constant tensions, i.e. dissonances which, however, are constantly resolved—yet whenever a tension seems to abate, a new dissonance is again at work.

The principle continues. In bar 9 the first group ends. Here the viola group dwells on E, the tone from which it started. The composer uses this point of repose to let the timpani and xylophone, as in an interspersed flash, sound the initial dissonance (F-sharp—B—F) again. Immediately, however, the B is once more resolved into C. At this moment the second violin enters on an emphatic G-sharp, taking over the main melody from the viola. The basic harmony is now: F-sharp—C—E—G-sharp, or in other words, the original chord of the seventh is expanded to a chord of the ninth. In bar 13 a new point of repose is reached with the main melody dwelling on B, which the composer uses to interpolate the initial dissonance once more. (Here the timpani can spare the B which is now heard in the violin.)

Thus this music presents an over-all picture of uninterrupted dissonances, of which the most ardent atonalist could not wish more. This becomes all the clearer when, by looking at the example, one further realizes that the detail of the melodic line which connects the corner notes is not only in the chromatic (rather than in the diatonic) vein, but itself consists almost entirely of additional, very emphatic dissonances. Yet—and this is fundamental—these dissonances are not thrown into the design, as though no consonances existed in music. For because of the curvature of the melodic line all these dissonances appear, as it were, conscious that it is their destiny to be resolved—even if the resolving note itself becomes immediately a new dissonance, or even if the resolution never takes place at all.

Before comparing this structure with a counterpart from the atonal realm, a brief digression is in order so that we may examine precisely whether and how the phenomenon of 'moving tonics', previously described as one of the characteristics of the pantonal concept, can be observed in the Bartók example. It was pointed out that here F-sharp represents the foremost tonic, from which as a basis the leading harmonies are developed. One could well call F-sharp the tonal centre of the group. However, as the harmonic combination in the first bars consists of F-sharp—B—F, changing to F-sharp—C—F, it cannot be avoided that tonical relationships uniting F-sharp and B as well as C and F will sound through. And the systematic transparency of this continuing pattern leaves no doubt that this was the effect the composer intended. The F-sharp, especially, oscillates beautifully between being the tonical basis of the melodic-harmonic main course and, at other moments, the overtone of the B—a moving tonic in the truest sense.

How different is the structural concept and, indeed, the innermost spirit of the design in the next example (Ex. 7 on p. 144)!

74

Here the opening group from No. 1 of Anton Webern's Five Movements for String Quartet, op. 5, is quoted. This work was written before the twelve-tone era, yet it represents an almost perfect example of atonality in music.[1]

The piece starts like a signal with two soaring intervals in fortissimo: a minor ninth, notated as an augmented octave (C—C-sharp) followed by a major seventh (F—E). The E is three times emphatically repeated, now accompanied by a chord. This chord has a thematic rather than a harmonic meaning. In its combination of C-sharp—C—F—E, it expresses the first two motifs, now in chordal contraction. Then a melodic sequence to the first bars (shaped as a kind of contrary motion to the preceding intervals) is sounded in the first violin. These figures are accompanied by chords in the lower voices. In bar 3 the second violin plays a canonic imitation to the first violin's passage (now with changed rhythmical accentuation).

This canonic imitation enters on E, while at the same moment the first violin has D-sharp, thus here too expressing a major seventh. The entrance on the motivic interval, however, is the only 'harmonic' connexion between the two canonic voices. Apart from this motivic nuance the intervals formed by the encounter of the two canonic lines are left entirely to chance. In two or three instances they are consonances, in all others violent dissonances. This in itself would not matter. But what, perhaps, is problematical in this design, is the fact that there is no structural idea behind this interplay. The dissonances do not point to any consonances, and the few consonances are haphazardly brought about by canonic coincidence. Yet the canonic lines are not *invented* in such a way as to insure a structure which would make the distribution of dissonances and consonances an intentional

---

[1]As stated on several occasions, our purpose in introducing any example for analytical examination is never aesthetic adjudication. What is to be demonstrated is merely the antagonism of the various trends contained in the compositions in question—trends which leave their imprint on the musical picture of our age. Of course, in a higher sense, no artistic explanation can and should ever be entirely neutral. Thus it is unavoidable that certain nuances will reveal where in this polarity of tendencies the author's sympathies lie. This, however, does not prevent him from expressing his appreciation of the musical and technical qualities in works such as the present example.

pattern. The composer simply decided to imitate the leading voice *somewhere* and the 'canon' came into being. The accompanying chords in the lower voices are—harmonically speaking—in the same random vein, adding nothing to the compelling quality of the design.

In the next bar another canon in miniature follows, this time in four voices, where each voice enters a minor ninth below the other. But here too, as throughout the whole piece, the interplay between dissonance and consonance, even in the transformed way seen in the Bartók example, is missing. And with it any vestige of tonical relationship. Thus all the structural wonders displayed in the score remain formalistic. Yet there cannot be any doubt that all this is obviously the composer's clear idea and intention. A musician of Webern's skill could have created an entirely different picture, had he so wished. What he strove to delineate was a musical world in which 'emotion' was expressed merely by colours and dynamic shades, while any relationship binding the lines together (apart from motivic reiteration) was avoided—thus a world of tonical non-relationship: atonality.

Tonality through Pitches

An architectural device which is frequently used within the stylistic concept of pantonality and which there attains specific significance, may be called *tonality through pitches*.

Now in the widest sense every kind of tonality is based on pitches, for tonality is a phenomenon creating structural units by centring a phrase, a group or a whole piece on a basic note from which the group usually begins, with which it ends and to which the ear relates each part of it. And since the compositional essence of a note is its pitch, one can state that tonality is based on pitches. However, this statement is more true with regard to melodic than harmonic tonality. For harmonic tonality, though also based on tonical pitch, nevertheless operates through the inevitability of harmonic progression forcing a line to return to the tonic rather than through the binding strength of the tonical pitch itself. And we know that in harmonic tonality a group in C can conclude on

G or E, or even on an independent 'deceptive tonic' just as effectively as on C itself.

In melodic tonality the tonical force is, quite naturally, more
directly bound to the recurrence of the tonical pitch, as was
shown in the Biblical example quoted in Part One. Yet even these
'melodic tonics' of old folklore can change, can modulate, without
depriving the tune of its tonical flavour. The reader will easily find
many instances of this type of 'melodic tonality with changing
tonics' in almost any collection of oriental folk music. And in
modern music, from Debussy on, owing to an incomparably more
complex design, these instances increase in frequency.

To this modern type of 'tonality through pitches' we must
now turn. It is characterized by the fact that pitches which by
repetition and resumption become accented corner notes in the
compositional course can by this very quality assume a quasi-
tonical role, that is, can help a group appear as a unit and can thus
create form, even if the harmonic design of the group points to a
different tonical path or to no basis at all.[1]

For these instances the examples quoted in the foregoing chapter may serve as illustrations. In the Bartók example (on p. 142)
the F-sharp, as was demonstrated above, retains a kind of tonical
preponderance within the multitonical design and through this
the unity of the group is brought about. But this unity is intensified by the particular construction in which a certain arrangement
of pitches is several times reiterated. The constant return of the
high F and B above a ground of F-sharp and C, regardless of how
the actual melodic line has proceeded in the meantime, renders
the grouping of the whole section particularly transparent
through the force of the ceaselessly returning pitches themselves;
and this despite the fact that some of the notes in question have at
certain moments also tonical functions. The clinking of the high
xylophone which returns over and over again and which the
composer is very careful never to transpose to another pitch,
keeps the impression of unity very much alive, especially since it

[1]From a different angle and pointing to different effects, a related phenomenon is
described under the heading 'identical pitch' in the author's *The Thematic Process in Music*.

always occurs at decisive points, usually when one sub-group is about to be succeeded by another. If one looks at this design with a sense of form, one would like to predict that the movement will end with the same effect—which, indeed, is actually the case.

If the Bartók example shows the tonical effect of identical pitches that complement the fluctuation of tonalities, the Webern example presents the same phenomenon as a sovereign, no less impressive feature. For here, in the atonal environment, no ordinary tonalities support the quasi-tonical effect of these pitches. In fact, the whole first movement of Webern's quartet is in a sense architecturally held together by these identical pitches. A very subtle application of this phenomenon of 'tonality through pitches' binds even the first group (bars 1—6) together. For the emphatic opening through the fortissimo C—C-sharp, finds a counterpart in the bass of the last bars of the group, which express the reversion, C-sharp—C, in pianissimo but no less emphatically. Were the C-sharp—C transposed to a different pitch, no one would think even remotely of implying a relationship between the ending of the group and its beginning. But through the sustained pitch a unification, or at least an intimation of it, will not escape a musical listener. That this subtle effect was intended by the composer is proved by still more evidence. When two measures later the second theme enters (Ex. 7b), the most characteristic interval of the rising cantando phrase is again C-sharp—C. But the most emphatic effect of tonical pitch is seen in the concluding group of the piece (Ex. 7c), where the constant C—C-sharp (see brackets) runs through the whole design. Here we see an application of the phenomenon in its truest form. Were one to ask whether this is not simply a motivic recurrence, so common in any musical style, the answer would be that naturally it is a motivic recurrence, but one of a particular quality. For if such a motivic recurrence appears, for instance, in a classical piece, it is integrated into the harmonic design which returns to the original tonic. But here, in the atonal realm, the motif returns to its original pitch not by reason of a unifying tonic, but in spite of the lack of it. And this emphatic return of the motif at its original pitch creates the effect of an architectural unity somewhat reminiscent of the standard tonical recurrence. Then, however, as a typical feature of Webern the atonalist, a last, slightly strange effect is added. As though wishing not to endanger the atonal atmosphere by even a vestige of 'tonicality' brought about by motivic pitches, a pizzicato chord in pianissimo of different pitch is annexed, through which the hard-won quasi-tonical unity is annulled.

Returning to the phenomenon of tonality through pitches, the author hopes its nature has been sufficiently described in the foregoing examples. However, it should still be emphasized that such 'tonical pitch' is not just an occasional, a rare occurrence in modern music, but one of its basic, most characteristic features—in fact, one of the pillars of modern structural formation. Every modern composer is aware of it and applies it frequently. In the modern idiom a piece or a group in C, for instance, is very often not centred on the C harmony but on C—G-flat—C. If from there it progresses in its harmonic texture to various harmonies, and if only it finally returns to the C—G-flat—C with which it started, the listener will easily and unhesitatingly conceive the whole group as a quasi-tonical unit, notwithstanding the fact that no chords of the C key, and still less of the dominant, were included.

However, it should also be understood that 'tonality through pitches' is usually not the only structural idea through which a musical group is unified. It often merely forms one of the contributing factors that unify a complex multitonal fabric. The other factors are harmonic tonality, melodic tonality, crossing tonality, etc. It is through such tonical manifoldness that the compositional design finally assumes that very flavour of 'pantonality' which forms the essence of our inquiries.

A-Rhythm and Pan-Rhythm

It is logical that whenever a change in one sphere of expression takes place in music, this cannot fail to affect the other spheres. Thus it was only to be expected that the change which, with the advent of the modern style, took place in the harmonic-melodic sphere would also become apparent in the realm of rhythm. In fact, it is astounding how parallel in many respects is the evolution in the two spheres.

In classical music the basic principle of the rhythmical concept was a rhythm of symmetry. This rhythmical symmetry corresponded to the regular succession of tonical cadences on the harmonic plane. In the rhythmical realm the symmetry is brought about by accents. In the score these accents appear as bar-lines which, of course, are nothing more than an easy way of notating regularly recurring accents. A bar, or to use a more correct expression, a measure, contains two or three beats or their multiples—four, six, eight, nine or twelve. Sometimes, but comparatively seldom in classical music, five or seven (instead of two or three) are chosen as rhythmical units. Apart from the small groups, called measures and defined by bar-lines, larger groups are created by comprising several measures into a higher rhythmical entity, a so-called 'period'. In the classical concept, the normal period consisted of eight measures or, if notated in quick tempo, of sixteen or perhaps thirty-two measures.

All this, however, signifies only the basic principle of rhythmical formation. In practice this basic principle is greatly enriched by expansions, contractions and variants of all kinds. This enrichment can take place in two different forms.

First, the basic rhythmical symmetry is often modified by shortening or (more often) extending the eight-bar period. Regular eight-bar periods, except perhaps for main themes, do not occur very frequently in classical music. Secondly, and this is of even more far-reaching significance, the groups in the different voices of a composition are by no means always shaped according to one unifying rhythmical idea. Rather their rhythms often differ; in fact, the groups themselves often overlap, through which sometimes a fairly complex rhythmical picture may arise: a *second rhythm*, superimposed on the basic symmetry. In this sense a difference between metre (meaning the *basic* rhythm as expressed by time signatures and bar-lines) and rhythm in a *specific* sense (as expressed by phrasing and grouping) is established, though in common terminology an accurate distinction is not always maintained. In this connexion one must also remember that classical music is in great part much more polyphonic, much less based on 'accompanied homophony' than a widespread but inaccurate view would hold. Apart from some piano music—and even this only to a limited degree—the main body of classical literature, its chamber music and symphonic works abound in rich and genuine polyphony. And this accounts for rhythmical variety within a symmetric metre. For with melodic polyphony rhythmical polyphony often goes hand in hand.

Classical music received this particular type of rhythmical variety as a heritage from the music of the polyphonic era proper. For then, as the shapes of the melodic lines were much less tied to symmetry and accents, and the concept of bars was non-existent, the entrance of each new voice took place also in a somewhat similarly free manner, that is, unfettered by rules of symmetry and periodization. And classical music took over some of this 'freedom' into its otherwise stricter grouping, of course adjusting the technical application to its own language and style.

But classical music also introduced another form of rhythmical enrichment which was realized by a *third* rhythmical layer superimposed on the layers just described. The third rhythmical layer was brought about by complementing and often counteracting the basic symmetry through irregular accents *within* the phrases which form the second layer—a feature which was hardly known in the polyphonic era. These irregular accents, notated as accents proper, as sforzatos, tenutos, or in a wider sense even as crescendos or diminuendos, in short the whole dynamic palette, often supported and intensified the regular rhythmical picture but no less often lay outside of and even in contrast to it. Haydn and Mozart made ample use of such multiplicity of rhythm, while Beethoven led it to a peak, indeed, drew the highest structural—and emotional—effects from an abundance of often violent asymmetric counter-accents. From then on, in the romantic period, these constant counter-accents became a common device.

But the great change in the rhythmical sphere came with the

advent of modern music toward the turn of the century. In the harmonic-melodic sphere the main characteristic of the change was the abandonment of tonality. In the rhythmical realm it was a corresponding abandonment, or almost abandonment, of the concept of symmetry. And just as in the harmonic sphere the evolution moved in two fundamentally different directions, one stream towards atonality, the other towards pantonality, so in the rhythmical province a strikingly similar dualism of trends was to be observed. One trend tended towards an abandonment of the specific rhythmical impulse altogether, towards a kind of *a-rhythm*, the other towards an enrichment, an intensification and finally a true transformation of the old rhythmical idea, towards *pan-rhythm*.

Here we must go into some detail, as this part of the development has seldom been described. As stated above, the classical concept of rhythm was in essence a rhythm of symmetry, a rhythm of accents. In a somewhat allegorical analogy, one could say classical music was in a sense dance music or, at least, music conceived from a dance-like impulse. Of course, the actual, emphatic dance accentuation was maintained only in some more or less stylized dance forms, such as minuets, scherzos, etc., while in most other instances it was somewhat subdued, since an over-emphasis of the dance-like pattern would have cheapened the actual musical message. Such an over-emphasis on accentuation, moreover, was no longer necessary in well-shaped music, as the transparency of the periods and smaller groups was sufficiently assured by logical phrasing. To intensify this art of phrasing, in fact, to make it more complex, was, as described above, the chief means of endowing the composition with rhythmical variety.

Now, in one province of modern music—the atonal—such 'rhythmical variety through phrasing' was attempted by weakening, or even gradually abandoning, the underlying rhythmical symmetry. What then remained was a complex web of phrases, often well-articulated, yet without rhythmical impulse and finally without rhythm itself. The composers and commentators of the atonal school still called this web of manifold phrases 'rhythmical variety'. In fact, they emphasized that such designs represent the only true type of higher rhythmical formation, while symmetric accentuation of any kind expresses merely the outer, superficial symbols of rhythm in music. Such a view, however, is a confusion, at least in terminology. For rhythm as a musical phenomenon and sensation, is definitely and always centred on some regularity of accent. If the accents disappear, rhythm and rhythmical feeling evaporate, and what remains is a kind of musical *prose*. Let it be said that this is not meant as an aesthetic criticism of this a-rhythmic trend in music—just as in literature, poetry and prose are not in themselves yardsticks of artistic value. Indeed, rhythmically free or even a-rhythmical music can be traced back to a quite legitimate and noble historical lineage, such as toccatas and fantasies of previous periods, and farther back to much of the early religious recitative. What should be emphasized here is merely the fact that the part of modern music that abolishes symmetric accentuation entirely, inevitably also abolishes rhythm, notwithstanding the diversity or even intensification of phrasing retained in the design. Moreover, such extreme abandonment of rhythm, if applied too often and too thoroughly, as is the case in parts of the modern, the atonal production, entails some further consequences that cannot be overlooked.

First, our analogy of the artistic values of poetry and prose in music and literature, true as it is in principle, must be modified in practice. While in literature prose is the normal human language and poetry the expression at certain exceptional moments, in music almost the opposite is the case. Here rhythm is an eternal impulse, the normal state of expression, while a-rhythm is an interesting variant, suitable to a specific frame of mind.

There is another point of complication. For if this a-rhythmical type of music is applied, as it usually is, to a rich polyphonic design of diversified phrasing, it is very difficult to bring about a satisfactory performance, i.e. a performance in which the composer's intentions are brought home to the listener. Every musician who studies new scores, occasionally comes upon a kind of writing where—bane of the conscientious conductor—an array of divers tempo marks, fermatas, sudden ritenutos, and accelerandos meets the eye, all within a few bars, sometimes literally within one bar. (To which, since even in this way everything cannot be indicated by notation, lengthy footnotes explaining the meaning of the marks are often added.) The result is somewhat problematical.

In his book *The Orchestra Speaks*, Bernard Shore, a well-known member of one of England's leading orchestras, raises the curtain on some activities and trade secrets of an orchestra. In referring to the musical style here in question he stresses the surprising difference between the conductor's achievement during the rehearsal (when he obviously can concentrate on explaining and analysing) and during the actual performance, when he must depend on the music proper. Speaking of a conductor who specializes in this type of music "with a single bar of eight quavers over each of which there is a different indication", Shore adds: "With the most painstaking patience he did his best faithfully to follow the composer's directions, to the utter distraction of the orchestra; but when it came to the night, nothing seemed to matter very much, and all the hair-splitting went by the board."

This, then, conveys a fair picture of a-rhythm in action. No doubt, the loosening of musical symmetry represents one of the positive structural impulses of our age, as it frees the composer's imagination for an abundance of new effects. Yet carried to its extreme, it inevitably leads to an impasse analogous to the impasse in the harmonic sphere resulting from pure and extreme atonality.

But just as in the harmonic sphere only one stream of the modern evolution pointed to atonality, while another, broader stream pointed to something different and almost opposite, so too in the realm of rhythm, the trend towards a-rhythm was counteracted, and indeed conquered, by a trend towards richer rhythmical patterns, towards pan-rhythm. As we referred to Debussy as a beginning and symbol of a new positive trend in the harmonic-melodic sphere, we may analogously point to Igor Strawinsky as a beginning and symbol of the new spirit of rhythm.

What are, technically speaking, the new rhythmical patterns which Strawinsky introduced?

The author recalls some years ago attending a lecture in the music department of a New England university on the evolution of rhythm in modern music. Embedded in a mass of scholarly and aesthetic explanations, the gist of what the speaker maintained was the following: While the time units in classical music were two or three plus their multiples, with an occasional five or seven included, modern music would add eleven, thirteen, seventeen and perhaps higher cardinals as quite natural rhythmical elements. One could easily imagine what fascinating combinations would be in store for us if, for instance, a rhythm of thirteen sixteenths were contrapuntally juxtaposed to a rhythm of seventeen dotted eighths. The lecturer, no less than the audience, became truly intoxicated with this colourful prospect. Unfortunately, however, the evolution has not at all confirmed such fantasies. At any rate, what Strawinsky initiated, and what has since become the general trend, points to something quite different. Ever-higher and more complex numerals were not introduced as elementary units, *but the familiar, simple elements were combined to ever-richer, more diversified and more complex patterns of rhythm and accentuation.*

Turning to Ex. 8 (on p. 146) we may tabulate a succession of time signatures from a typical Strawinskyan design. What we here encounter are not units of an order such as thirteen, seventeen, nineteen and intricate combinations of these elements, but the old units of two, three, or four, now in new patterns of alternation, in new arrangements. Sometimes a $\frac{5}{8}$ bar is interpolated to enrich the picture, but the rhythmical substance remains, at least theoretically, simple. Yet through the clash of different orders of accentuation, such as two or three $\frac{3}{8}$ bars, followed by a $\frac{2}{4}$ or a $\frac{3}{4}$ bar, again followed by a $\frac{5}{8}$, the design sounds even today, almost half a century after it was written, highly stimulating and exciting. An ear adjusted to the classical rhythm might be inclined every once in a while to skip or interpolate an eighth beat, in order to restore the 'regularity' of accentuation. Yet to the listener who is accustomed to the rhythm of Strawinsky (or for that matter to that of Bartók and many other moderns) the pattern in question conveys a definite and quite natural rhythmical idea. However, fully to comprehend the nature of the effect here involved, one should not forget that all these rhythmical irregularities are in this piece introduced only *after* a regular $\frac{2}{4}$ rhythm has been definitely established at some length. Thus the spirit in which the irregularities are applied reminds one somewhat of the way in which dissonances are used in the pantonal domain. Just as these dissonances, notwithstanding their uninterrupted occurrence, must be understood as a deviation from consonances, the asymmetric rhythm must be understood as a deviation from an underlying regular rhythmical pattern, although this regular pattern may for long stretches hardly appear at all.

Thus Strawinsky dispensed with the classical symmetry, without abandoning the classical rhythmical impulse itself. In fact, he enriched and intensified the classical idea of rhythm—somewhat in the way in which Debussy disposed of classical tonality, while still retaining the tonical phenomenon and the tonical spirit as such. The composers from the a-rhythmical camp, on their part, abandoned rhythm itself by trying to replace its grouping quality through elaborate phrasing. In contrast, Strawinsky, in the more emphatically 'rhythmical' parts of his compositions, at times gave up phrasing and shaping almost entirely, relying at such moments solely on rhythm and accentuation—a fact which some commentators are inclined to see even as a kind of deficiency. Whether this should be so regarded or not, is not under discussion. Here Strawinsky's positive achievement should be stressed, which in creating a new concept of rhythmical structure has already influenced and will continue to influence whole generations of musicians.

Thus the basic point demonstrated so far is the bipolarity in the evolution of rhythm: one stream tending towards dissolution and abandonment of rhythm, the other towards its enrichment and transmutation into higher rhythmical patterns. However, corresponding to events in the harmonic sphere, further development in the rhythmic sphere produced—and even more clearly here—astounding symptoms of a rapprochement of the two fundamentally divergent trends.

All these tendencies point to an endeavour to preserve the idea of rhythmical symmetry but at the same time to transform it into higher, more complex formations or, in other words, to blend regularity with irregularity. The simplest patterns of this type are the so-called 'alternating rhythms'. While the old idea of symmetry was expressed by a continuous succession of $\frac{2}{4}$ or $\frac{3}{4}$ units, new and easily comprehensible patterns can be developed by an alternating scheme of, for instance, $\frac{2}{4}$—$\frac{3}{4}$—$\frac{2}{4}$—$\frac{3}{4}$ etc; or $\frac{2}{4}$—$\frac{3}{4}$—$\frac{3}{4}$—$\frac{2}{4}$—$\frac{2}{4}$—$\frac{3}{4}$—$\frac{3}{4}$—$\frac{2}{4}$ (this pattern could also be notated as a $\frac{5}{4}$ rhythm with alternating accents).

But more complex patterns born of similar impulses emerge in recent years. Some of the twelve-tonists—to be exact, the younger, less orthodox twelve-tone composers, who are swerving more and more away from pure atonality—seem also the first to surprise one through new and particular patterns of rhythm and symmetry. Boris Blacher, for instance, employs a device of 'variable metre'. Blacher suggests "arithmetical series like 2, 3, 4, . . . 12; a summation series 2—3—5—8—13; series formed by permutation, etc."[1] In some instances he develops a fairly effective and even easily comprehensible rhythmical design, especially when he restrains his theoretical imagination within the limits dictated by his inherent musicianship. Were he, however, to carry out his theoretical patterns without hesitation, then indeed a state almost similar to that predicted in that university lecture would soon be reached—a state *in abstracto*, for in the performance such a play of numbers would anyway not be perceivable.

There can be no doubt that in the coming years more attempts at creating new rhythmical schemes, new patterns of metre and accentuation will spring up. Regarding this whole subject, however, one point should not be overlooked: namely, that skill or lack of skill in notation plays no small part in expressing, or sometimes obscuring, the (rhythmical) idea intended. Here the difference between rhythm and metre assumes increased significance. For rhythmical patterns, even intricate patterns of irregular rhythm, must not always be apparent in the surface notation.

[1] Rufer, op. cit., p. 178.

Luigi Dallapiccola, whom we quoted previously in another context, states almost naïvely that "Wagner . . . one of the greatest innovators in musical history, never showed any special concern for the rhythmical factor. In his whole gigantic output he only once used a $\frac{5}{4}$ bar. . . ."[1] However, intricate rhythms are by no means restricted to the use of frequent $\frac{5}{4}$ or $\frac{7}{4}$ metres. The metrical picture, as expressed in the notation, indicates only a part of the rhythmical idea of a composition. It is true that in many instances rhythmical complexities must appear in the metrical pattern. But this is not necessarily always the case. Modern composers are often inclined to scorn outer clarity and readability in their scores. One has the feeling that they sometimes even rejoice in a rather bewildering, if not confusing rhythmical picture. However, the more versatile the modern composer becomes in the handling of rhythmical diversities, the more often will he at times succeed, not in avoiding rhythmical difficulty and complexity entirely, but often in hiding complicated combinations, brought about by rhythm-forming accents, behind a comparatively simple metrical design. In fact, an effective and easily readable rhythmical and metrical notation, in spite of possible underlying rhythmical diversity, today becomes an art in itself.

Many new, far-reaching rhythmical ideas may also be established by the other type of compositional formation, *that tries to combine different rhythms contrapuntally*. Of course, if carried out in a purely mechanical manner, this method would hardly amount to more than a kind of 'rhythmical polytonality'—figuratively speaking. But if the composer manages to integrate different rhythmical concepts into a higher unity in an inspired and convincing manner, truly novel effects of real 'pan-rhythm' could result.

One interesting and early example of contrasting rhythms which are juxtaposed can be found in Hindemith's Piano Concerto, 1924 (Ex. 9 on p. 147).[2] But even before Hindemith, several

---

[1] Rufer, op. cit., p. 179.

[2] Of course, a far earlier, highly ingenious polyrhythmical structure is found in the first act of Mozart's *Don Giovanni*, where three orchestras play simultaneously in different metres.

highly impressive samples of cross-rhythms, in which entirely different patterns of metre and accentuation sound simultaneously, were realized by the American composer Charles Ives. Some of these pieces do not represent mere experiments but are true visions of new rhythmical realities. (A more general description of some of Ives' structural innovations is given in Ex. 10, on p. 150.)

In fact, rhythm in general plays an important role in the works of American composers. Perhaps as a result of an old affinity to jazz, Americans are even in their present, almost jazz-free compositions inclined to indulge in striking, sometimes bizarre, but often effective, new patterns of symmetry and rhythm. But also outside of America, though naturally applied in different ways in individual countries and schools, the search for a new musical rhythmical impulse becomes a foremost ingredient in the works of many composers of today.

Of course, one has to realize that here we come dangerously close to the point where creative invention may reach or surpass the borderline of the physically possible. For if these diverse and divergent designs are not very competently, almost cunningly, shaped, both with regard to invention and notation, they can easily become stumbling blocks in performance. In its last essence this problem will not be solved until, in a distant—or perhaps not so distant—future, musical performance, or at least a part of it, will have become independent of the limitations which instruments and performers, symbols of life though they are, still impose on it. But of this more anon.

Pantonality and Form

In discussing rhythm, our deductions had necessarily to deal with the question of how compositions are grouped and what role rhythmical units, such as measures, phrases and periods, play in a work's structure. This brings us to another important, though perhaps somewhat vaguely defined, conception: namely, the conception of *musical form*.

What lies behind the idea of form in music, and in what way

has the introduction of modern music changed this idea and its practical application?

Before answering these questions, some general remarks must be interpolated. For the term 'form' in music covers two different fields of technical operation.[1] In the first place, form is created by the working of the motivic and thematic forces, by the development and formation of a whole piece from the variation and treatment of a few motifs and themes. In fact, form in this sense is the truly important factor in creating the structural beauty and depth of a composition.

But there is also another idea of form at work in music. Form in this second sense is manifested by the way in which a work is grouped and divided into parts and sections. The technical operations here involved endow a work with its outer, architectural form. This is what musicians usually think of when they speak of form. In the following pages, whenever the term is used, this 'outer' form is meant, at least as a point of departure; although we may later return to the more general concept which includes the inner idea as well.

Having clarified our terms we may repeat our initial question: How did the introduction and evolution of modern music influence the concept of form, and what changes did it bring about?

There is a strange, almost amusing development to be observed. Classical music, or perhaps still more, classical musical theory, operated on the basis of *schemes*, such as the sonata form, rondo form, etc., according to which the compositions were built. Naturally, these schemes were never strictly observed and they were relaxed more and more in the romantic and post-romantic period. The reason for this is that classical form, of which the sonata form was the main representative, was developed in a certain parallelism to *harmonic* architecture. Therefore, when the classical concept of harmony was loosened, the schematic forms also became less valid. With the dawn of modern music, then, composers and theoreticians raised their voices ever more strongly towards an abandonment, if not a complete ban on the old

[1] With regard to this dualism see also the author's *The Thematic Process in Music*, p. 109 a.ff.

'forms'. It is without question, they held, that the new harmonic concept also demands new patterns of form; and that these new patterns will come into being out of the musical idiom itself.

Therefore, everyone watched expectantly for the coming of a new pattern of form.

But although the modern idiom became more and more outspoken and even branched out into various techniques and styles, interestingly enough, *no new general schemes of form emerged anywhere on the compositional horizon.*

What was it that prevented the expected 'forms' from materializing?

To understand what lies behind all this, one has first to realize that the core of classical form is *the principle of grouping as such*, not a certain, specific way of grouping, not the schemes. The specific schemes, which even in the classical period were not always strictly observed, are merely individual instances, subject to change in different periods and in different compositional orbits—while the principle itself is an almost timeless device. It is actually 'form'.

Yet in the course of time, due to long usage, *the principle had become confused with the schemes.*

Consequently when, with the advent of modern harmonic design, it became increasingly clear that the old schemes which were based on the tonic-dominant progressions were no longer tenable, musicians thought they had to look for new schemes as a new principle of form. And they were obviously disappointed as no new schemes made their appearance.

With regard to this problem, a few further words should be added. The classical principle of form was based, first, on the method of grouping just described; second, on the resumption of a theme or section which had already appeared earlier in the same composition. The re-entrance of familiar shapes (as for instance in the repetition or recapitulation of a sonata) unites the parts between in one architectural entity. These two comparatively simple devices, first the method of grouping, second thematic resumption, constituted the whole source from which the concept of outer form in the classical period was developed. All schemes, such as the sonata, rondo, minuet and the many others, meant merely specific applications adapted to certain thematic, harmonic and rhythmical types of composition. Therefore, when in the modern era the harmonic and rhythmical designs changed, the schemes also had to be adjusted accordingly. But merely adjusted from case to case—for since in modern music manifold harmonic progressions and rhythmical patterns, rather than one unilateral harmonic basis (such as the tonic-dominant relation), generated the compositional design, no single scheme could emerge to correspond to such variety. Yet, although no specific scheme made its appearance, the deeper principle of form did not disappear—that principle which in classical music generated the tonic-dominant schemes and which in modern music enables the composer through diversified ways of grouping and various kinds of resumption to develop *any 'scheme'* he desires. In fact, this principle constitutes now as ever the basis for creating form in music.

But the atonalists, just as they shun regular symmetry and emphatic grouping, usually do not like thematic resumption either. This, of course, does not mean that their music is formless. For it may be deeply entrenched in that other type of form, motivic consistency. Of course, whether such motivic unity can completely make up for lack of certain aspects of outer form as achieved by grouping, remains debatable. With regard to a piece such as the first movement of Schoenberg's Third String Quartet for instance, even the listener who finds the idiom itself attractive may remain in doubt as to the unequivocal disposition and balance of the sections, both from an architectural and dramatic point of view. He might hardly be able to say why all this, architecturally speaking, must be as it is; why, for example, the end comes when it does. To repeat: inner form, thematic form, is by no means missing in this type of music, but merely a definite pattern of outer, architectural form. In contrast, the modern non-atonalists, shall we say the pantonalists, since they are not bound to a specific structural principle as are the twelve-tonists, have infinite possibilities at their disposal from which all thinkable kinds of 'form', in fact schemes of form, can be drawn. The fourth movement of Bartók's Music for String Instruments, Percussion and Celesta, for instance, from the third movement of which we quoted on a previous occasion, shows the following scheme: A, B, A; C, D, E, D, F, G, A. Moreover, towards the end of the movement the main theme of the work's first movement is resumed, now expanding the original chromatic version into a diatonic variant. Perhaps less concentrated than the simple tripartite sonata scheme, yet in the end no less logical, is this freer and more complex pattern which corresponds so well to the manifold tonical relationships in Bartók's piece.

The younger generation of twelve-tone composers, however, just as they drew nearer to all other aspects of pantonality, also approached this type of freer, yet well-organized concept of form. Thus we have in this realm, too, the familiar antagonism: the true atonalist almost abandoned 'form' as a means of architectural grouping;[1] the others, striving towards pantonality, rather intensified the sectioning, the grouping of their compositions, setting up individual schemes for almost every work.

There is a further feature of significance in which at least part of this same antagonism became observable. Classical music made use of a structural device, the application of which became almost a rule: namely, the familiar device of 'themes'. Themes in the classical sense were musical thoughts of a certain length which, through their quality, position and emphasis, became important architectural pillars within the composition, the grouping of which they helped to make more transparent. In this way they also conformed more or less with the harmonic course, as expressed in the over-all cadential scheme. The genuine atonalists, however, at the beginning of their movement—and there were

[1] It was only a natural consequence of this tendency that composers of that style, owing to the architectural vacuum just described, resorted in the dawn of atonality to strangely small-sized compositions. Schoenberg refers to the "extraordinary brevity" of these works, adding that at that time neither he nor his pupils were conscious of the reason for it. "Later I discovered", he states, "that our sense of form was right when it forced us to counterbalance extreme emotionality with extraordinary shortness." (*Style and Idea*, p. 105.) The emphasis on the fact of this "extraordinary shortness" is justified. The attempt, however, to explain it as having been forced by the necessity "to counterbalance extreme emotionality with extraordinary shortness" remains debatable.

genuine atonalists almost only at the beginning—shunned markedly distinguishable and lengthy themes, since they evoked too many memories of clear-cut divisions connected with tonical construction. But when in the later evolution the twelve-tone composers, as previously described, departed farther and farther from atonality, themes inevitably reappeared and, with them, all the familiar devices of grouping, resumption, and in a sense even the old 'schemes'. Naturally, the symphonies, sonatas, suites, which today every modern composer, be he atonalist or not, produces, are not conceived in accordance with the tonic-dominant scheme. But the over-all principle, though now varied in countless ways, is still alive, and there is no more talk even among the ultra-radicals that any new 'form', any new pattern, is in the making that would replace, say, the sonata form.

Nevertheless, the stream of evolution does not stand still in the sphere of form. There are currents and eddies of various kinds which press to the fore. One current is centred on the question of a-thematic music.

A-thematic music should not be confused, though it sometimes is, with music without themes. A-thematic music is music which is not based on thematic or motivic consistency, but music in which the course develops, so to speak, freely, without using the affinity of thematic shapes as a structural bond. It is noteworthy that both the great pathfinders of modern music, Debussy and Schoenberg, at times toyed with the idea of adopting a-thematic formation as their principle. Both, however, finally rejected the idea, Schoenberg by introducing the twelve-tone technique, which on the contrary carried the principle of motivic consistency to its extreme; and Debussy by dismissing the matter, at least in practice, though there always remained a tendency in his music occasionally to loosen the thematic bond. Some years later the Czech composer Alois Haba came out strongly, perhaps with more theoretical than practical success, for a-thematic composition. But not until recently did a similar trend emerge in the music of a wider circle of composers. The author, in showing a certain interest in this idea, hopes not to disappoint readers who followed his earlier treatise, *The Thematic Process in Music*, with kindly approval. It may seem strange that after having written the strongest possible plea for the necessity of thematic logic in musical composition, he does not dismiss the whole subject of a-thematic composition from the outset. And indeed, his attitude has not changed. If he is certain of anything, it is that thematic consistency as an artistic *principle* can never vanish from compositional formation.

Yet all this does not mean that in some individual compositions or in parts of them the line could not, even repeatedly, be interrupted through new, seemingly unconnected thoughts. If skilfully applied this may at times even produce a specific, highly effective style of expression. Examples of a similar character can occasionally be found in some high-ranking literary products of the last decades. In recent musical attempts, moreover, this method of temporarily dismissing thematic consistency is combined with new structural ideas.

To understand the problems posed by this evolution, we must first become clear about the technical aspects implied in the concept of a-thematic music. Even the simplest deliberation shows that the term can never be accepted in its extreme, literal sense. A-thematism must remain a tendency, an approximation, somewhat analogous to atonality, which according to our previous description must also remain a tendency that can never fully reach its goal. Absolute a-thematism is an unthinkable idea in music. For it would mean the complete exclusion of any unifying agent, the complete lack of any connection between the parts of a composition, in fact, in its final sense, even the negation of the composer himself as a structural organizer. Thus the degree to which a-thematism is possible in practice is signified merely by the exclusion of the more or less traditional thematic and motivic mechanism and by the substitution of some other connecting method, be it a structure based on elements of pure rhythm, phrasing, or—and this is especially interesting—on any serial idea, that is, the twelve-tone or any other row. Accordingly, a-thematic designs, contradictory as it may seem, emerge frequently in compositions that at first would appear to be the most tightly-knit motivic configurations, such as music written in twelve-tone or in any other serial technique.

In compositions of this type the organization of the composer's thoughts is not attempted by starting from any theme or motivic phrase, but rather from a 'sound-formation' (the term 'chord' would not accurately cover what is meant) and by developing its inherent possibilities into wider groups. The basic formation is thus the structural impulse for the whole group and is replaced only by the next formation, which itself is somehow related to the first.

We may turn to a concrete example, the opening bars of Pierre Boulez' Piano Sonata No. 1 (Ex. 11). Bars 1 to 4 obviously constitute the first group, divided into two sub-groups, A and B. Although at first glance one might believe this to be a twelve-tone design—and it is quite possible that the composer considers his work as conceived in this vein—a closer examination reveals something different. The first sub-group (marked A in the example) rises from F to an expressive D and, significantly, also concludes with D—a D which is accentuated by a *sffz*. Through this a kind of tonality—of course, a rather atonal 'tonality through pitch'—unifies the group. The following group (B), answering the first, even concludes with a full restatement of the opening: F-sharp, D, E-flat, F, or in numbers, as given in the example: 1, 2, 3, 4. Thus a structure of intensified identical pitch emerges. The last D, as a half note, at the same time forms the beginning of the reintroduced opening series, now heard in retrogression: 9, 8, 7, 6, 5, 4, 3, 2, 1. In this way all three opening groups together (A, B and C) are framed by the F-sharp—D, and thus form one unified whole, notwithstanding that the F of the last sub-group reaches out into an annexed prolongation of one bar.

What should be made plain by all this is the so to speak tonal impulse behind the atonal design and the fact that it was drawn from an a-thematic serial idea. Here we singled out merely the elements pointing to the tonal impulse, ignoring all other structural ideas which might be present. Also the aesthetic question of whether the composer was or was not able to evolve a convincing artistic message through his theory may be left out of the discussion.

Turning to another example, quoted from the concluding group of Benjamin Britten's opera *The Rape of Lucretia* (Ex. 12), it should be understood that this example is by no means introduced for the sake of any parallelism or similarity to the first but rather for the sake of utter contrast to it in every stylistic, structural and even ideological respect. Yet being two extremes, the Boulez and the Britten quotations may demonstrate most emphatically into what divergent regions the departure from older structures can reach. Thus pantonality may even indicate a synthesis of tonality and atonality—a phenomenon about which we shall become more explicit later.

For, if the Boulez example shows how extreme atonality can, at least in part, be annulled within and by its own atonal fabric, the Britten example demonstrates how an almost completely tonal fabric can by the intensification and diversification of its own texture create something quite different from tonality.

At the first glance, the Britten example would seem as strikingly tonal as the Boulez seemed atonal. Yet Britten's tonality almost disappears if one follows the inner contours of the lines and does not take the chordal expansions too literally. In this vein even the lengthy pedal point on C would almost give the impression that it is not so much a harmonic basis out of which the upper harmonies grow and diversify (as are pedal points in classical music) but is in great part merely a colourful background destined to produce ever new sound combinations with the upper layers. These upper harmonies, or rather 'harmonic melodies', almost invariably overlap, so that one enters while another still sounds and thus create hidden atonal relations and effects between each other and the bass. Yet a kind of undefinable supertonality is still maintained. And as for thematism, while an almost traditional thematic shaping is expressed in the lines of the choruses, the orchestral 'accompaniment' in its magically austere instrumentation adds free, almost non-thematic colours.

The Boulez and Britten examples, be it repeated, were juxtaposed here merely for the purpose of demonstrating how trends toward pantonality can evolve from contrasting structural principles. Here we are at one of the crossroads, indeed, perhaps at the focal point of our investigation. On the one hand we have a typically atonal and a-thematic concept (as in the Boulez example), on the other hand a typically tonal and thematic one (as in the quotation from Britten's opera). Yet each leads to designs that transcend finally both tonality and atonality as well as thematism and a-thematism. Evolution, to be sure, seldom follows one straight line but usually seems to spread out into various divergent paths which only much later effect a reunion.

This trend from tonality and thematism toward something beyond them, without first passing through the purgatory of atonality and a-thematism, can be observed in a greater part of the contemporary creative production. It began with some British and American composers, notably Vaughan Williams and Aaron Copland. Copland in some of his works, as for instance in his Third Symphony, has introduced a style which is much more personal than that found in his more popular, half-programmatic orchestral poems.

In some parts of this work structural ideas are indicated which open new vistas of compositional formation. Ex. 13 is a quotation from the beginning of the symphony's second movement. The opening fanfare by the horns points to F major, though the B-natural (which is also maintained in the subsequent sforzato of bar 3) adds a different, so to speak modal, colour. In bar 7 the line rises to F-sharp whence, after some motivic intensifications, it finally (bars 11 and 12) concludes in the B-natural. Thus the whole group can be heard in two ways: either tonally focused on B-natural, in this case C (over-all pitch of the first four bars) represents a kind of Neapolitan sixth, followed by F-sharp (dominant) and B-natural (tonic); or, the line may be regarded simply as departing from F major and leading ('atonally') to B-natural. After a few excursions a new thought enters (Ex. 13b), which in essence is an inversion of the opening fanfare. In Ex. 13c, then, a kind of second theme is introduced, a rather charming blending of the opening theme and its inversion. (This emphasis on thematic consistency is a paramount feature in this phase of compositional expression, as we shall demonstrate later.) This theme is in F again, and with an augmented expression of it the movement also concludes.

Though the example does not convey more than an indication of the trend in question, it is noteworthy, because it shows the idea in rather a transparent way. While Strauss, Mahler and their generation expanded tonality often to an intense degree without ever loosening its discipline, Copland, the pioneer of the American evolution, is, though perhaps simpler than they, at the same time freer, less inhibited, and thus the seed is sown for later development. And in pursuing this trend towards more intricate patterns further, a whole generation of younger, often extremely gifted British and American composers may be seen enriching the musical picture of our time. The farther this process develops, the closer the two contrasting principles seem to become: the one starting from the tonal-thematic concept, the other from the atonal, a-thematic one. In a later chapter we shall refer to this evolving synthesis more concretely.

However, there is one point which seems essential with regard to this whole subject—a point which now as we gradually approach the end of our inquiry will become more and more important in our argumentation. It is the conviction that among all these experiments, those which are primarily based on negation, *have a chance to survive only if a way be found to integrate them into the general musical whole.* Unless these new techniques themselves become part of the universal musical 'law', they will remain less than short-lived, even if they were hailed by those who introduced them as the last word in artistic achievement. The avant-gardist, of course, thinks that all that was before him became obsolete with the first stroke of his pen and that the year One has come again. Such fanaticism may sometimes even be fruitful, as it may open, perhaps not new artistic empires, but interesting provinces. Even these provinces should be explored with caution.

As Paul Henry Lang once said: "A radically new style can never destroy the older one . . . armed rebellion in the arts is seldom successful."

This statement is valid for the specific concept of a-thematic music, which can only become a living, if limited, compositional idea by being made, paradoxically, a part of the over-all thematic principle; it is valid for a-rhythm, which can only prevail by becoming a part of pan-rhythm; for atonality as a part of pantonality. And it is also valid for a vast and entirely new domain of musical expression which has sprung up in recent years and about which we shall soon speak in some detail.

The Evolution of 'Colour' in Music

In our preceding explanation on form we had to deal with that part of the artistic idea which is expressed purely by the design of the composition, regardless of the various types of sound through which such a design may be brought into being. These types of sound are usually referred to as musical colours, by analogy with the fine arts. Since the different colours are brought to life by musical instruments, the art of producing colour is based on the technique of applying and combining these instruments, i.e. on the technique of instrumentation. A musical work can be instrumentated for a soloist or for a small (chamber) group, or—and this has become in many respects the most important type in the last two centuries—as a composition for a whole orchestra. Therefore, the development which the orchestral palette has undergone during these centuries may be discussed below.

After all that has been said about the evolution in other spheres, it would seem almost a logical consequence that in the realm of orchestration an analogous dichotomy might be expected: one branch corresponding to the elements which produce atonality, the other tending to the diversified possibilities of pantonality. Alluring as such a schematic analogy might seem, it has the defect that it does not conform to reality. The familiar bipolarity cannot be detected in the domain of musical colour. Yet an examination may still yield some interesting results.

Classical orchestration, though thoroughly organic, with the smallest detail meticulously worked out, was at the same time in essence rather simple. The strings, as the technically most developed and most flexible instruments, had also to carry the main burden of the compositional course, the woodwinds accompanying and occasionally entering with a contrasting theme, while the brass supported by the timpani completed the design. The picture was enriched in the later classic and following romantic period, when the different orchestral groups rose to a more equal footing. This trend was intensified with the advent of modern music, where often a tendency became visible to raise the wind instruments to an even higher position than the strings.

Of course, the widening and intensifying of the use of the wind instruments was only one specific feature within the general tendency to increase the range of available colours as such. In this sense, composers from Berlioz on gradually drew upon the entire compass of the orchestral palette, especially including the highest and lowest registers of the individual instruments. In fact, extreme registers sometimes became the main source from which the colour plan of a composition was developed.

Within the general trend to enrich, to increase the compass of possible colours and combinations of colours to the utmost, two opposite tendencies became observable. However, as indicated above, these two opposite tendencies can by no means be identified with the two contrasting directions towards which the evolution moved in the harmonic and rhythmical spheres. Rather it was a question of individual taste that determined the side towards which a composer tended. Moreover, a different spirit of orchestration is occasionally observable in different works by the same composer.

In trying to describe the two different principles of orchestral painting, one could say: the one principle attempted a height of expression by obscuring the role and individuality of the single instruments and groups of instruments, fusing them into a stream of vibrating and almost indistinguishable colours; while the opposite principle strove towards the highest colour effects by preserving and even intensifying the role of the orchestral individualities and groups, organizing the orchestra almost like an assembly of human personalities.

However, be it repeated, this antagonism does not correspond to any general stylistic polarity, nor in most instances can a definite principle of orchestration be ascribed to all works of one composer or even to all parts of one work. The reason that such ascriptions usually do not conform with reality is that the differences mentioned, which are very clear in principle, are hardly ever applied fully in practice, as they are often changed and combined according to the composer's momentary intentions. There is no doubt that the creative vision of Latin composers is less centred on polyphony and therefore would seem to tend more towards transparency in colour than that of their Germanic counterparts. Yet looking at works like Debussy's *La Mer* and Strawinsky's *Petrouchka* or, on the other side, Strauss' Symphonic Poems and Schoenberg's Five Pieces for Orchestra, op.16, one would hesitate to state with certainty which of the two principles is applied in any of these compositions. Rather one would be inclined to say: both principles were at work in each of them. Thus the existence of the two principles is mainly of theoretical importance. Yet they do represent real forces that direct the composer's mind at different stages of his work.

One trend in the evolution of musical colour, however, proved steady, universal and irresistible during the last centuries: namely, the trend to widen the range of the colour spectrum, to increase its possible nuances and combinations. Indeed, this trend would long ago have transformed the orchestral palette into a medium of far higher diversity and effectiveness, had it not been for the limitations imposed by the nature and physical mechanism of the musical instruments. The composers, abetted by ingenious performers, tried to overcome these limitations by various tricks of virtuosity.

How the colour spectrum can be broken up into countless shades, even within such a limited instrumental range as a string quartet, can be seen in the previously quoted example from

Webern's Five Movements for String Quartet (Ex. 7). Even within the first one and a half bars we hear three fundamentally different colours: regular bow, col legno and pizzicato. The initial augmented octaves (C—C-sharp in the second violin and 'cello) are played in one bow, carrying the dynamic mark *ff*, followed by a crescendo. The responding major sevenths (F—E in the first violin and viola), which are also rhythmically differently placed, are marked pizzicato. Then follow three col legno chords in *fff*. Again the viola and 'cello continue with some pizzicato chords bearing within one and a half bars the dynamic marks *ff*, *f*, *p*, *pp*, followed at the end of bar 3 by an arco chord in *ppp* on which an accent is imposed. The following canon in miniature (bar 4) is to be played sul ponticello, again in *ppp* to which a diminuendo is annexed. All this within the first four bars and a similar picture prevails throughout the whole piece. The result is often very effective; no less often, however, one effect neutralizes the other.

But apart from the infinite possibilities of diversified sound which the string instruments provide, we can in general find in modern scores all kinds of special effects, such as pizzicato glissandi of the strings, glissandi of the overtone series in the horns, timpani glissandi, etc. etc. Some of these devices certainly add to the enrichment of the palette, while others may look more impressive in the score than they actually sound in performance.

Perhaps, however, music is *de facto* on the eve of a fantastic upsurge, entailing a never-dreamed-of widening of the colour spectrum, which would render superfluous the earlier attempts just described. The following pages will tell us more about these possibilities, which at a later date may perhaps initiate a truly new chapter in music history.

The Electronic Wonder

As is generally known, the technological discoveries of our time also brought a host of devices into being which surprised the world with a variety of new sounds. Not only new sounds of a specific type, such as any age adds to the existing stock by the introduction of new musical instruments,[1] but a whole new category of sound. This development started in a sense with the invention of the gramophone and radio, to which in recent years the tape recorder with a host of affiliated electronic devices was added. In this way not only the fixation and later reproduction of any kind of sound and noise were enormously facilitated, but the possibility was established of changing colours and pitches at will, of increasing or reducing tempo and dynamics, in brief, of transforming a piece in any imaginable (or even unimaginable) manner.

It is not surprising that music or, first of all, the musical industry hastened to make use of these possibilities. Today in radio and film, as in all kindred spheres, electronic devices not only form one of the foremost agents of sound production, but in considerable part also account for the style and even content of the music produced.

Even art music has partaken of this development. Composers cultivating electronic music emerged particularly in France and Germany and to a lesser extent in America, and were soon divided into several sects. As was to be expected, the most radical of them declared that electronic sound represents the only true music of our age and that all previous music will soon constitute but a primitive, as it were, pre-historic stage that must eventually disappear from artistic practice.

However, the music produced by the 'electronists' hardly justifies such proud claims. And anyway, for the present the main interest of all parties concerned seems to centre on the various technical possibilities of bringing about this new world of sound and on its physical-acoustical properties rather than on its musical content. It fits into this picture that those who present us with this music are often engineers rather than actual composers, or teams of engineers and composers. Yet, since our present study is not a survey of the different events in contemporary music but is con-

---

[1]However, at the same time one should remember that most of our modern instruments are, at least in principle, of ancient origin. They have accompanied Man through the millennia, though they were brought to their present perfection only during the last centuries. This is a fact of significance, for it shows that the assemblage of instruments used today is not the result of a chance development but of a natural growth and artistic logic—cf. Curt Sachs, *A History of Musical Instruments*.

cerned with the unravelling of the principles which give the broad streams their direction, we shall not go into the detail of this whole development.[1] Yet there is one aspect in this sphere of electronic music which is of interest, indeed of great interest, to our subject: there can be no doubt that because of the technological progress initiated by these electro-musical experiments, the composer will in time to come have at his disposal *both an infinite, uninterrupted series of pitches and an infinite, uninterrupted series of musical colours.*

To be sure, electronic musical practice is still very far from this state, though some composers of the electronic school behave as though it were already reached, or at least just around the corner. Yet this goal cannot be even approximated until instruments, or shall we call them machines, appear on the market—yes, on the market, not merely in someone's richly endowed laboratory —machines on which the composer can easily transform into reality any musical design that his creative imagination demands: any polyphonic combination of infinite pitches and infinite colours. Only in ten, twenty, fifty years, or more, then—and not until then—may a new chapter be added to the already extant chapters in the fascinating story which music history represents.

About the situation at this future stage some remarks should be added. Although we do not know what actual and detailed consequences such a stage would produce, there are nevertheless a few points which can be stated without fear of losing ourselves in speculation.

In such an electronic future, when the composer may 'play' his composition into his 'instrument' for later direct reproduction, the idea of performance may change. Though it is very unlikely, at least for many decades to come, that performers will disappear, they may assume new functions, leaving to the composer more

[1]However, it may be noted that the French-American composer Edgar Varèse was one of the first to point in this direction and thus is sometimes referred to in Europe as the 'father' of the whole development. Moreover, the American composer Henry Cowell began experimenting as early as 1911, and in his compositions, among them the fascinating *Banshee*, he introduced sound effects through non-electronic media which in their colour and direction clearly point to the musical domain which today is attempted through electronic equipment.

responsibilities in some matters but taking over some of his tasks in others. The composer, at any rate, will have the possibility of transforming into musical reality combinations of a structure so complex that today he would not even be able to notate them. Then, one might surmise, the time for a-thematic composition, for a-rhythm and atonality would have arrived. Here, however, comes a surprise. For thinking this matter through, just the opposite seems to be true. And this leads us to one of the salient points in our whole chain of thought.

Whenever that age of infinite pitches and infinite colours may come—be it by means of electronic devices or in any other unforeseeable way—many conceptions which today appear as self-evident properties of the daily musical routine will become obsolete or even vanish entirely. The ingenious chromatic scale of our well-tempered system may not escape. *But there is one element which cannot become obsolete, because it is based on a natural, unchanging phenomenon. This is the overtone series and the harmonies deriving from it.* Whether the future musician will wish to make use of these harmonies is a different, purely aesthetic question; just as we see that they are not much in use today. But as an eternal directive, as a pillar of musical construction, even though their actual expression be avoided, they cannot be dethroned. Here Lang's previously quoted words of armed rebellion being seldom, if ever, successful in art, are especially pertinent.

Today the avant-gardists of musical electronics rejoice in the thought that there will be no boundaries to their desire for change and iconoclasm. In reports from European musical festivals in which electronic music begins to play a part, it is almost amusing to observe how the 'old gentlemen of modern music', Schoenberg and the twelve-tonists included, are looked upon with benevolent joviality, like friendly uncles, who are somewhat out of date. Yet the electronic movement is not even advanced enough to make its adherents recognize wherein their problem lies. This problem which, because of the participation of complex technological elements, is more intricate than any musical problem of past periods, is centred on the question of *how to integrate this music and all that it implies into the stream of the musical evolution.* For here the danger of plunging into the void is especially acute. The wider, the more boundless the musical compass, the greater will become the necessity to bring order into the diversity. In the vastness of its future territory, music will inevitably have to choose between dissolving into chaos or organizing the infinite. It is the same antagonism that we see today warring between the contrasting forces of atonality and pantonality. And with this, after some perhaps lengthy yet necessary excursions, we return to our actual subject.

IV

The Role of Pantonality as a General Synthesis

In the foregoing deductions we tried, first through direct description, later by more indirect methods, to develop a picture of the types of compositional formation which we have included under the term pantonality. Yet in spite of our endeavour to view the problem from all possible angles, there may, even in the minds of those readers who followed our explanations with some interest, have remained a slight feeling that the core of our thesis, i.e. the technical nature of pantonality, was not delineated in sufficiently concrete terms. Compared to the way, for instance, in which the idea of twelve-tone composition was introduced into music, complete with an exact set of rules, the concept of pantonality as here described may seem to be of a somewhat generalized, almost indefinite character.

Such objections, however, though they may seem justified in point of fact, are nevertheless based on false premises. Quite apart from the fact that this writer would certainly not feel himself authorized to issue rules for a new method of composing, the two conceptions are of an incommensurable nature. 'Composition with twelve tones' refers to a technique, i.e. a compositional category perhaps somewhat comparable—though the comparison is only partially applicable—to the fugal technique. Pantonality, on the other hand, is a general compositional concept, as is tonality or atonality. It cannot be defined by a rigid scheme or by a set of rules, but can be made comprehensible only by describing its nature and effect, by examining its divers facets and qualities. Pantonality remains a tendency, an approximation, as were tonality and atonality. There was never absolute tonality demonstrable in any musical composition, nor absolute atonality; they are but concepts, as is pantonality—*yet by virtue of being concepts they were no less real, for they constituted the directions which determined the course of music.*

Here it may be permissible to interpolate a personal recollection. At a time when the twelve-tone technique had been in use for only a few years, the author asked the following question of a young but well-known composer: "What caused you to shift from your previous style, in which you were obviously able to express yourself successfully, to the new technique?" After a slight hesitation the following answer was given: "It was not a question of being able or unable to express myself sufficiently. I realized— and this seemed alluring to me—that in no other type of musical writing would I have to overcome such 'resistance of the material' as in the twelve-tone technique. That was the reason I turned to it."

Subjectively, this statement—which certainly was entirely sincere—pointed to a highly ethical artistic attitude. For it showed an inner conviction on the part of the composer not to let any sacrifice stand between himself and his goal. Yet coming closer to the core of the problem, one could wonder whether the desire to overcome technical difficulties is really an inherent part of the creator's task. A composer should certainly not shun difficulties but there is no reason either why he should search for them. The question which alone seems artistically important is whether the result conforms with his creative vision, rather than how he attains this result.

It may be helpful to return to our comparison of the twelve-tone technique with the fugal technique and try to evaluate some facets of this analogy. The first fact that comes to mind is that fugues, or for that matter passacaglias, are difficult only from a beginner's point of view, while viewed from a higher aspect they actually represent easier methods of composition. They demand less of the composer's imagination, since the pattern of their structure is in a sense predetermined. Naturally, this does not imply that there are not many fugues and passacaglias of highest rank. But the achievement lies in the fact that the composer was able to produce real works of art, not because of the technical patterns he had to fulfil but almost in spite of having to adjust the flow of his imagination to a given technical scheme.

In view of all this one begins to wonder whether a composer turning to the twelve-tone technique as 'the most difficult way of expression', does not harbour deep in his heart the hidden hope that here for once he would be on safe ground; that here he would be less exposed to the danger of occasionally not knowing how to give his thoughts a definite form, in fact, sometimes to let 'form' replace thought. This desire for protection, this fear of perhaps being lost in the ocean of modern musical expression, was certainly at least one of the reasons why quite a few composers turned, and still turn, to this technique.

Conversely, it is significant that in recent years these same composers show an ever-increasing tendency to loosen the rigid application of the technique, in fact, to make of it something which is almost the opposite of its original idea. Earlier we described the trend in detail; and if to this is added the observation previously advanced, that in the realm described as pantonality all kinds of atonal or twelve-tone shapes may be and are included, one cannot but speak of a rapprochement of both spheres. Indeed, the undeniable fact of such a rapprochement constitutes one of the most significant symptoms in the musical evolution of our time. But it also presents one of its most delicate and intricate problems, for its consequences can only be understood, and a possible solution found, by taking into careful and unprejudiced consideration all the divergent forces, general and technical alike.[1]

In the first place one must not forget that atonality and the twelve-tone technique, notwithstanding all that may be said against them, have enriched the compositional range with a whole world of new possibilities. They have made available to the composer a host of new melodic types, new harmonic combinations and, for that matter, new rhythmical and structural ventures,

[1]Viewed from the aspect advanced above, one of the most interesting musical spectacles of our age may assume a new and increased meaning: namely, the astounding renaissance of British music during the last decades, its almost violent re-entrance into the international musical arena after a lengthy period of relative creative inactivity. For this renaissance took place as a blending of the most opposite musical impulses of our time, yet without yielding to any of their extremes. British music from the beginning of its new phase marched in the forefront of the modern movement, at times even of its radical wing, but the goal was, aesthetically speaking, synthesis, not isolation; structurally speaking, integration, not atonality.

which otherwise might never have come into being. The opening up of this new world of expression, together with the hope that in this new world one could operate on a firm structural ground, attracted many composers to the twelve-tone technique. That by applying this technique, even in the most modified form, one cuts oneself off at the same time from many spheres of expression, is the reason why these same composers try to change the rules of the technique, and why today few of them consider it an exclusive way of composing but prefer to work alternately in twelve-tone and free style. For as long as the technique is maintained at all, even in the most modified form, there will always remain vast compositional territories which the composer cannot even approach. Pantonality, on the other hand, can of its nature embrace any atonal expression and can make it a part of its own planetary system of multiple tonalities. Indeed, as a state of fluctuating tonical relationships, pantonality can endow atonal shapes with a new meaning, make new melodic types into new melodies, new harmonic combinations into new harmonies, and even make a-rhythmical and a-structural ideas become expressions of a higher oneness.

In the light of all this it is not surprising that contemporary scores of the twelve-tone and of the pantonal type at first glance often seem not too different. Both seem above all to radiate away from the tonic-dominant concept. And the similarity may appear all the stronger in instances where the twelve-tone work tries to expand beyond its own orbit into some tonal domain, and when pantonal works include as many atonal thoughts as possible within the design. Nevertheless, and in spite of all this, there remains a tremendous difference between music which develops tonal aspects on a higher cycle, though it may in part derive from atonal lines (as does pantonality) and tonally unrelated music, though it may be modified by compromise (as is today most of twelve-tone music).

Indeed, the difference, even if on the surface it may not be conspicuous, is fundamental *both in principle and effect*. For pantonality works according to a basically free principle, not tied to any pattern of formation. Whatever atonal, twelve-tone or other serial features the 'pantonal' composer may include in his fabric, he includes them merely when he feels they express what he wishes to say at that moment and he immediately discards them whenever his creative intention calls for some other type of expression. In contrast, the twelve-tone composer, whatever compromise he may admit, whatever freedom from his rule he may permit himself, always must remain conscious that the principle towards which his ideas are dedicated calls for a fixed structure, for a 'mechanism'—though it be a mechanism with numerous possibilities, one which he may even break at will.

The Great Structural Dilemma of Contemporary Music

In this antagonism, therefore, between atonality and pantonality—an antagonism which, though decreasing in compositional practice, has not yielded an inch in principle—one of the main problems, one of the main dilemmas of contemporary musical construction becomes apparent. It is a dilemma with which every modern composer is faced, whether his music be of the serial type or in free style. The twelve-tone composer, as was described in detail in preceding pages, finds a firm structural basis in his ever-recurring row, *but in this very firmness he is often tempted toward a construction without inner harmonic meaning.* No such scheme dominates the shaping of the free-style composer. He, however, is faced with the opposite danger *of diffusing his thoughts in a design without a clear structural basis regulating it.* In classical music this basis was provided by the cadential scheme and by thematic coherence. Both these regulating elements seem to have become more or less ineffective today, at least in their old forms of application. How they therefore have to be replaced by new patterns of application, in which the original spirit comes to life in new combinations, may be shown in two last examples.

We quote first some groups from the Piano Concerto by the French composer André Jolivet (composed in 1950). We choose this work with its brilliant orchestral colours as a sample of an idiom which, as far as the degree of tonality is concerned, may be considered as fairly illustrative of the free modern style. Of course, in the example on p. 156 only the most essential voices are quoted. To facilitate comparison with the full score, reference is made to various sections by numbers (given in parenthesis) which are to be found in the score.

The opening group is given in Ex. 14a (on p. 156). An *auftakt* soars up and releases a strongly accented chord. The chord's harmonic constitution is a complex one, yet its main impulse seems to be centred on D, the dominant of G, to which as a harmonic centre the whole movement gradually turns. That this is so, is borne out by all that follows. For while this harmony is sounded in the piano, the first violins and trumpets play the opening melody, the first *theme* of the work. And this melody, too, is centred on D as a kind of 'melodic tonic'. The theme is accompanied by a chord played in harmonics by the other strings. The notes of this chord (B-flat—E-flat—F-sharp—A) are taken from the basic piano harmony just described, and together with the remaining D—A—D form that complex harmony on which the whole group is focused. And here is the decisive point: this central harmony and the thematic melody crystallize into one unit. Not only is the D the basis for both the harmony and the melody but all the successive corner notes of the melody coincide with notes of the sustained harmony. We may trace this note for note. The melody starts with D which, as just described, is also the focal note of the harmony. In the next bar the strong note of the melody is E-flat, which is contained in the harmony. In the following bar the strong notes are E-flat first, then A (played by the trombone), which is also contained in the harmony. In the next bar the strong note is B-flat, which also is a part of the harmony. It is interesting to note how consciously this whole idea is developed. For in bar 4 where the trombone enters, G-natural (first violin) would normally have been a strong point of the melody, but since this note is *not* contained in the harmony, its entrance is delayed by syncopation and, instead, the A (which *is* contained in the harmony) is sounded by the trombone. All this shows how in good modern music complex harmonies can be used without resorting to any law of the row or the like, and still be centred on a structural basis. The melodic and harmonic concepts of this group are truly one, and it would be hard to say which formed the main impulse.

In bar 7 the line departs from the D and descends to C (bar 8). This chromatic descent is taken from the beginning of the theme. If we regard the initial group as representing the dominant of G, the harmonic pattern in the next bars (8 a.ff.) seems to be IV (C—E-flat) followed by V (F-sharp—D)—though one should be cautious in applying such terminology to this modern design.

At this point rhythmical accents are introduced which, gradually supported by a lavish array of percussion instruments, lend a characteristic colour to the whole work. This course, with variants and extensions, continues for some time, to which at (2) (see score) a part of the opening theme provides a charming counterpoint in the *pp* of the strings. After a reiteration of the opening (4) the basic tonic G is finally reached at (5). Here a new melodic line rises in the oboe (Ex. 14b), a 'continuation' of the opening theme, derived from this theme's melodic material. Again the melodic and harmonic courses merge: the notes forming the 'dissonances' in the piano accompaniment are again taken from the melody. Only the basic G has a purely harmonic value.

At (8) the section of the second theme starts (Ex. 14c). The harmonic point of departure is again the G in the bass. But soon the design rises in the melody of the piano to a shape which must be regarded as clearly C-sharp minor. Yet since the accompanying strings complement this melody by an elaborate polyphony, the whole design, notwithstanding the inclusion of this feature of traditional tonality, does not convey the slightest suggestion of a break in style. This second theme is entirely different from, even in contrast to, the first. Significantly, however, its main melodic phrase (G-sharp—C-sharp—E—D-sharp—C-sharp) nevertheless is found to be a transposition of the basic contour of the first theme (bracketed as *a* and a^1 in the examples).

The second theme is worked out to a full section with diverse intercrossing tonalities, whereupon the development section (12) starts. Its beginning rises from G as the basic tonic, yet is once more interspersed with different tonalities.

This section finally leads to the coda (23), the climax of which is reached at (33) and (34) when finally no less than five themes combine in one rare, kaleidoscopic, yet at the same time most transparent, design (Ex. 14d). It is worth while to follow the courses of the five themes.

1. The first violins in unison with the first trumpet blare what is now the main theme, developed in various transformations from the opening theme;

2. The second violins and the third trumpet bang out the 'continuation' of the first theme in a ponderous rhythm;

3 and 4. From the 'cellos and double basses the two 'coda themes' sound, which were first introduced at (24);

5. In addition to all this, the movement's beautiful second theme is heard in the bass of the piano, supported by the horns (34).

Although clearly tonal as well as clearly atonal shapes emerge within this mass of sound, and although the movement concludes in an almost outspoken G minor, the final effect is neither tonal nor atonal but something quite different from both. The reader who does not balk at studying the score, of which only a very scanty indication was given here, will soon realize the purpose of this analysis. Here a compositional design is developed which in its polyphonic web and texture may at first glance seem as if it were patternless and almost arbitrarily conceived, yet in reality is centred on an unequivocal structural basis, though the composer's imagination is never hemmed in by any rule or scheme. And what makes this achievement possible is the fact that both harmonic and melodic ideas are in this work equally conceived from a unifying thematic impulse.

How a similar goal is attempted through a different method will be shown in the following and last example. May the author once more be permitted to quote some passages from one of his own works, Three Allegories for Orchestra?

Again the example is a kind of reduction in which only the essential design is quoted. Ex. 15b (on p. 160) shows the work's opening section. The chordal groups in bars 8 and 11 shine out through the instrumentation, which is centred on harp, celesta, piano and bells. In Ex. 15c some inversions, extensions and variants of these two chords are given, *for from the idea latent in these two basic chords the whole work is developed.*

Here some contrasts to the twelve-tone technique should be noted from the outset: first, the fact that the two basic chords contain one identical note, the E, and accordingly could contain even more identical notes in other examples; secondly, that in addition to inversions, contrary motions and the like, all kinds of *free variants* of the original idea are also applicable. However, in common with the structural idea of the serial technique, here too, both the melodies and harmonies are developed from a basic musical thought, expressed in the specific work by the two chords. Yet such adherence to the chosen structural basis *is here not a law but merely a general architectural directive.* The main themes are developed more or less as close variants of that structural pattern, but there are many connecting phrases in which the original idea is altered and even adorned with some new shapes.

Having indicated some general principles we may follow their application in Ex. 15b. The motivic idea inherent in the two basic chords can already be traced in the melodic course of the opening bars (1—6). For here from the strings and winds the combination A—E—B—F is heard, while bars 9—12 spell C—G—C-sharp together with F-natural (in the bass of bar 12), thus expressing two transposed variants of the basic chords.

Is there any vestige of tonality expressed in this shaping, and if so what is it? Almost every detail of the melodic contour is decidedly atonal. Nevertheless, if the ear connects any of the corner notes in the design, shapes based on melodic tonality ('tonality of pitches') emerge, which are centred on, and aim at, A as their goal. For instance: A (bar 1)—D-sharp (bar 7)—A-flat (11)—G (14)—A (15); or by connecting a lower melodic line: A (1)—E(4)—B(5)—G(9)—F-sharp (10)—F(12)—E-flat (14)—A (15).

In other words, all lines converge on A but in different, independent ways.

The two quotations that follow (Ex. 15d and Ex. 15e) are from the second and third movements of the same work. Ex. 15d quotes a fugue theme in allegro, while in Ex. 15e the beginning of the third movement is given, which is of a lyric or, if the forbidden word is permitted, almost of a romantic character. Different in mood and structure from the first movement as these two examples are, they are nevertheless built from the same chordal idea in an equally 'tonal-atonal' vein.

As indicated earlier, it was the purpose of many of our last examples to show that, quite apart from the serial method, music can be developed on a solid technical basis, even after the classical scheme has been abandoned. Schoenberg, who turned the abandonment into outright atonality, quite logically searched for some substitute that would replace the relinquished ties. He thought he had found this substitute in the twelve-tone technique. But in another evolution, composers from Debussy on searched for a solution in a different direction. Starting from bitonality and related phenomena on the basis of an ever-closer unification of melodic and harmonic ideas these composers developed a state of higher tonalities, of crossing tonalities, from which gradually an entirely new structural concept evolved: pantonality.

Of course, in this study, atonality and pantonality had to be described as the two stylistic antipodes which they actually were according to their historic origin, their technical design and their artistic ambitions. But if the evolution continues according to all indications presented by recent developments, it may during coming years become one of the specific tasks of some future theoretician to trace the changes and new functions which the diverse expressions of the serial technique (twelve-tone and otherwise) will assume *when they are applied within, and as parts of, a free style.*

Thus in spite of all fundamental differences in principle, musical practice works for a rapprochement. As numerous examples from very divergent musical provinces have shown, recent, even utterly contrasting, musical styles often have one trend in common: they part equally from unconditional tonality and unconditional atonality, endeavouring to create something new, a third concept. Here pantonality's highest and final function becomes visible: *as the great synthesis within the musical tendencies of our age.* Of course, in their pure forms tonality and atonality constitute two contrasting, two irreconcilable principles. But as was shown in detail in the preceding pages, if atonality retains its dogma in name only; and if tonality evolves into that higher state where the cadential circle is no longer the frame in which the expression is embedded but where, instead, a multitude of tonical relationships intensify, counteract and annul each other, so that finally their spirit rather than their mechanism is a compositional directive, then tonality and atonality may wondrously interpenetrate and pantonality becomes the great unifier. It may unify tonality and atonality and, in its highest emanations, even combine all three— tonality, atonality and itself, pantonality—into one universal style of organic freedom.

In general, we can observe an indication, perhaps more than an indication, of this tendency towards a synthesis of contrasts in one of the most conspicuous, yet little discussed characteristics of the modern style—and we speak in this connexion of 'style', fully aware of the dangers that the use of this equivocal term often implies. It is the fact that there is on the one hand hardly a period detectable in history in which one can observe such an abundance of different, often contradictory, idioms side by side, as in the music of our era: expanded tonality, modality, polytonality, atonality, twelve-tone technique, neo-classicism, neo-romanticism, matter-of-fact style, exoticism, machine music, electronic music, etc. etc. Incommensurable categories are intentionally placed side by side in this list, for in the last analysis each of these trends includes some aesthetic as well as technical and even chronological features. Yet from all this diversity one common denominator, one unifying sound rings through: the true musical language of our time.

In all this there may be included positive as well as negative factors, on which no judgment one way or the other should here be passed. What should be stressed is only the astounding variety within a common search. Particular stylistic by-ways are thus emerging. First, a frequent tendency of individual composers to express themselves through distinctly different techniques, indeed, through entirely antagonistic musical vernaculars in different works and even in different parts of the same work. Also some specific shades in between the main roads of the evolution, as for instance a certain method of structural formation for which Nicolas Slonimsky coined the term 'pandiatonicism',[1] come into this category. The term refers to a principle of formation, applied by Strawinsky and others, in which tonality would reign in the vertical sense but where no corresponding tonal idea directs the horizontal succession.

Fascinating as all this non-uniformity appears, is it not a symptom of a desire for a more definite and unequivocal style of musical expression, hidden behind the glittering façade of this manifoldness?

Dimitri Mitropoulos, the conductor, once surprised a visitor with some original thoughts on twelve-tone music.[2] Briefly, what Mr. Mitropoulos hopes for seems to be the advent *of a kind of twelve-tone music filled with Ravel-like flavour and appeal.*

Such a thought may at first appear to be an amusing paradox intended to avoid the solution of an insoluble problem. But does it not in a charming and intentionally naïve manner express one of the most profound longings of our musical age? Do not all of us dream of music in which all the novel, intricate and violent features of the most radical creations of our time would still emanate the beauty and humanity of the perhaps simpler but more straightforward musical structures of bygone ages?

[1] See N. Slonimsky, *Music since 1900,* also referred to in the *Harvard Dictionary of Music.*
[2] As related in *Music Makers* by Roland Gelatt, A. Knopf, New York, 1953.

AESTHETIC EPILOGUE

AESTHETIC EPILOGUE

I

ROMANTIC ANTI-ROMANTICISM

IN the *Harvard Dictionary of Music*[1] a surprising sentence heads an important paragraph. The sentence is surprising for it contains a statement of so subjective a nature that one might expect to find it in an aesthetic monograph but hardly in a work of reference otherwise so reliable and objective as is the Harvard Dictionary. The sentence reads: "New music is, briefly stated, anti-Romanticism."[2] Indeed—as simple as that!

The statement is not only debatable but also inherently vague. First of all, the vast domain of 'new music' (however this term be defined) cannot be interpreted as controlled by any single aesthetic impulse. Secondly, serious difficulties immediately arise when one proceeds to analyse what musical romanticism as an aesthetic category really implies. For the terms such as subjectivity, emotionalism, etc., by which it is usually explained, are no more than tautological slogans, problematic in themselves.

If there is any aesthetic musical term which in the eternal dialectic process of the evolution has constantly changed, and is still changing its meaning, it is romanticism. And logically, therefore, anti-romanticism as an alleged contrast to a concept already vague in itself, is vaguer than vague.

[1] *Harvard Dictionary of Music* by Willi Apel, Harvard University Press, 1953.
[2] That this generalization is not just a casual remark but the expression of a systematic aesthetic view can be shown by further quotations. Whoever is responsible for this segment of the Dictionary's definitions, certainly went too far when he stated (under 'Expression'): "that among today's performers the most common fault is the application of a highly expressive treatment to non-Romantic music, such as . . . Beethoven." And further: "In view of all these tendencies nothing seems to be more important for the student than to learn to play without expression. Only the student who has learned to play Bach's Chromatic Fantasia or Beethoven's Appassionata in the most rigid way will be able to add that amount of nuances and shades which these works properly require." Ideas like these are not only out of date as they represent, at best, a reiteration of some aesthetic tenets of a quarter of a century ago, but they were in fact even then not more than faddish, theoretical formulations which no performer of rank ever followed.

Trying to disentangle at least a few of the complexities involved, some historical facts should be recalled. The term anti-romanticism sprang up in aesthetic discussions around the turn of the century as a wholesome reaction against certain types of cheap sentimentality which had taken hold of some parts of the musical production. It was directed against a number of composers and critics, then forming the majority, who fought the new style by declaring it dry and lacking in feeling. The modernists quickly struck back, not only admitting but boasting of that lack.[1] However, in continuation of this tendency which in itself may have been justified, not only sentimentality but any emotional undercurrent which enlivened a musical composition was finally declared taboo. Indeed, the development went so far that what amounted to a dogma was introduced, claiming that if a musical work were to have any personal appeal and create a direct impression on the listener, one could justly suspect it of being of lower artistic quality. Now it may well be true that immediate appeal does not always vouch for artistic profundity. However, one should not forget that lack of appeal does not prove it either. In this whole matter it would seem that formulations are used to divert attention from the real issue.

Certainly, obtrusive personal sentiment often conceals or, as the case may be, even emphasizes vulgarity of feeling and thought. Correspondingly, however, pure structuralism and 'objectivity' may mean the dehumanization of art. Musical shapes remain lifeless matter, unless by transcending their own nature they become part of Man's metaphysical heart-beat.

Of course, the truly problematic, almost grotesque character of the whole argument broke into the open when anti-romanticism

---

[1]Here Romanticism is of course understood as a purely aesthetic category. However, the term has, as is well known, a strong chronological connotation, as it refers to the music of much of the nineteenth century, from the later Beethoven on to Wagner and Brahms and even Bruckner and Mahler. In an aesthetic sense the controversy was later explained as that of subjective, emotional and non-structural music, as opposed to objective, non-emotional and structural. This seemingly factual distinction, however, is scarcely based on fact. The music of the great and even outspoken romanticists, such as Schumann, Chopin, Wagner, Brahms, is deeply centred on structure, while in certain modern works of the most anti-romantic type, as for instance in some of the so-called machine music, structure is reduced to a minimum.

became not only a refuge for lack of imagination and emptiness of expression but, astoundingly, during recent times even reversed its own meaning. For the tendency to avoid emotion became amazingly emotional, the factual attitude became personalized. Subjective, indeed romantic, expression crept into the neatly prepared structures and rows. Then, in the electronic musical experiments, an outburst of super-romantic, often sentimental sound filled the air.

Paradoxical as it may seem, this development is not without logic. For in atonality, anti-romanticism was a fitting aesthetic hiding-place for the lack of a positive goal, but it cannot be maintained in the wake of pantonality. Soon romanticism which in practical music has already made many inroads will also stage a theoretical comeback. This does not mean that the term as such will be resumed. New slogans will spring up and they may feign very different, even contrasting aesthetic goals. Such a pretence may seem all the more plausible because of the tremendous changes in the musical vernacular and in all media of musical expression that have taken place in the meantime. Still, the impulse behind the new slogans will not be much different from that of the romantic approach, as there are in art only a few basic categories—categories which constantly disappear and constantly reappear. In the final analysis all these aesthetic antagonisms, such as romantic versus anti-romantic, subjective versus objective, and the like, are but contrasts in terminology. Their meaning changes with every new wave. They are finally merely aesthetic vehicles, if not camouflages, for the only lasting antagonism: *vitality versus sterility*. Indeed, the highest artistic truth of these phenomena lies in the fact that all these trends come and go; that the truly creative genius who introduces them, and under whose impulse they may direct the compositional course of a whole generation, also implants within his own work the seed which will finally destroy them. The romantic and the anti-romantic camps will always each maintain that they and they alone are right. Yet they will both be the losers when music is the winner.

II

EACH TIME ENGENDERS ITS ART—ART GENERATES THE TIME

In the course of this study an attempt was made to draw a picture, if still somewhat summarizingly, of a new compositional concept which so far has not been the subject of theoretical investigation. Yet there is no doubt that many composers of today must be conscious of its existence, or at least apply it instinctively. Pantonality was chosen as the linguistic symbol for this new trend, to denote its fundamental independence from both atonality and tonality, which are so often regarded as the only possibilities of the evolution. Although, therefore, in the light of our deductions atonality and pantonality represent divergent principles, and pantonality was thought to be the trend that would finally emerge as the more comprehensive and more enduring idea, our presentation was nevertheless careful not to picture atonality as a negligible or inartistic movement. For not only was it the evolutional purpose of atonality, paradoxical as this may appear, to prepare pantonality, but finally even to become a part of it, although atonality may in this process have to forfeit some of its own nature. And this refers not only to atonality as a specific principle but to all its technical components: to its harmonic and melodic elements, its rhythmical characteristics and even to its aesthetic parallel, anti-romanticism. It constitutes one of the fascinating experiences of our musical age to witness this development by which one compositional concept provides the other with much of its technical material and in the process changes its very nature and direction. The inquiring mind may well ask whether these startling events correspond to some general changes in the spiritual structure of our time.

During the last decades there has been a tendency to understand and describe the development of the arts not as an independent process detached from the general evolution but as a part of the broader stream of spiritual and social events through which human history is manifested. Music in particular, since its medium of expression is only loosely connected with the objects and happenings of the outer world, although it exerts a strong appeal on the human mind, was long considered as an almost isolated domain. Its aesthetic demands and the conditions of its structural mechanism were thought to follow their own laws, which seemed to bear no relation to any non-musical experience. Today this view has been entirely changed and a number of enlightening studies have taught us to realize how, often even to the point of the most subtle nuances, music is influenced by its time.

If this influence of the time on its art is today a generally accepted fact, there is another stream of forces which is much less recognized, although its effect in moulding history may be no less far-reaching. It is the stream of forces by which art influences its time.

That the day's happenings recur in our dreams is a familiar story—but do not dreams also shape reality? If so, where is the final reality?

Our own age is an extraordinary one. In the several thousand years of human civilization there was never a time so full of promise yet so threatening. Of course, if we look soberly back into history, we must admit that the world was always torn by confusion and catastrophes of all kinds. But today this whole state has reached such a peak that our human species is now literally threatened with extinction. Although this is the general picture, the majority of people, still desirous of happiness as individuals, look with a mixture of fear and bewilderment on a world which they themselves collectively have created.

Out of what does this overflow of destructive forces come?

The fact will not have escaped attentive observers that our present state of excess and the evaporation of fixed values was already foretold some decades ago in a specific realm: the arts. At that time, of course, few people, least of all the artists themselves, took this seriously or, to state it more accurately, thought of any relationship between nihilism in art and in the real world. If murder and deceit, insanity and death became the main impulses from which the subject matter and spirit of artistic creation were nurtured, this was, it was thought, because here the most interesting and most profound problems of the human psyche were rooted. Could perversion and crime or the orgy of dissonance harm anyone as long as they were realized only in the dream-world of art?

Life soon gave the answer in a horribly affirmative way. Sins in which one rejoices in the inner domain of the mind cannot but finally become outer realities. In the writings of Lewis Mumford,[1] one of the most stimulating and sincere thinkers of our time, one may find an abundance of facts pointing to this frightful parallelism.

Thus it cannot be wondered at, that we observe many people who, searching for a rescue from this terrifying state, renounce modern art as a whole and, in fact, would like to impose a moral or even a legal ban on it.

The problem, however, is not as simple as that. Not only is such a return to the pleasures of the Victorian age artistically undesirable, since actually it would elevate the non-creative and mediocre to the central role, but, above all, it is utterly impossible. A turning back of the rolling wheel of history was often attempted but never effected.

Indeed, what is necessary is not the way back, but a deeper understanding of the nature and purpose of art and its material, and of their relationship to life. We will never be able to change reality as long as we cannot change our dreams.

The Ivory Tower

Today when the dreams have become shudderingly true and when reality has robbed them of the last vestige of charm which even perverted dreams have, the artist, realizing the ineffectiveness of further horror, sometimes tries to withdraw into esoteric

[1]See for instance the chapters 'Renewal in the Arts' and 'Irrational Elements in Art and Politics' in Mumford's study *In the Name of Sanity*, Harcourt, Brace and Company, New York, 1954.

isolation, into a kind of reactionary modernism, where quasi-scientific ambitions replace creative impulses and keep the uninitiated out of his bleak sanctuary.

Of course, when observers warned that modern music, if it were to continue on its present road, would find itself banished to an ivory tower, the aestheticians of the alleged avant-garde promptly picked up the gauntlet. The modern composer, they declared, must not only realize that the ivory tower is his lot but he must strive for it and rejoice in it. Such a separation of art and life, they held, may actually prove one of the great catalysts of the coming age, through which human evolution will mysteriously progress into a higher and unknown existence. In the highest achievements of musical art, such as many of the works of Bach and of Beethoven's last period, this state, according to that opinion, was already anticipated.

In a sense, such an attitude is almost understandable as a reaction against the contrasting contention that genuine art must have an immediate appeal to everyone, that the 'masses' are the final judge of artistic value. Unfortunately, however, such a belief is no less questionable or, at least, is a vast over-simplification. But its being questionable does not render the theory of the ivory tower more convincing. For the ivory tower which surrounded some of the truly great art of the ages was not sought by the artist but was imposed on him by the outer world. The artist suffered from this agonizing isolation. He may at times have been forced by inner necessity to create shapes for which he was condemned to an ivory tower; the impulse, however, behind such creation was then invariably a longing to break down the tower, to prove that he was unjustly sentenced.

But we must return to our subject and to its specific domain. In the musical iconoclasm of our time everything which seemed firm and unassailable in the universe of sound appears shaken to the ground. Phenomena which were thought to be of timeless validity are not only questioned but declared non-existent: thematic thinking, tonical coherence, rhythmical symmetry, as well as the antithesis: consonance versus dissonance. In a sense such a dethronement may be a blessing even for the further development of these phenomena themselves, as it will help to prevent their petrification. And when, as certainly as day follows night, they re-emerge, rising in a new palingenesis, they may have changed their surfaces, their forms and technical roles, but not their innermost nature and purpose. Pantonality, already in the making, is a sign of their rebirth. And as for dissonance, it is the most wonderful, the most fundamental of all devices on which musical creation has thrived for centuries and will thrive again and again, ever increasing in importance and degree. Yet it owes its very existence only to the fact of being a deviation from, and thus a part of, consonance, of that higher harmony, indeed reality, of which music and life itself are but symbolic expressions.

MUSICAL ILLUSTRATIONS

MUSICAL ILLUSTRATIONS

Melodic Tonality

Ex.1 Jewish Chant (according to Idelsohn)
(a)

(b)

Mozart: *The Magic Flute*
(c)

THE TONALITY OF DEBUSSY

134

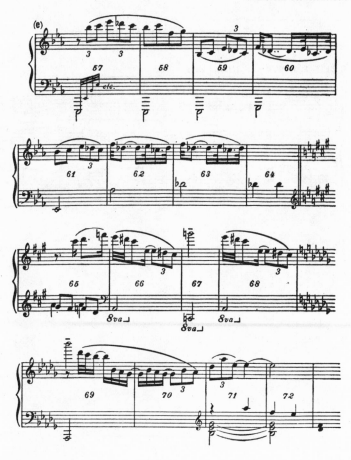

Debussy: *La Cathédrale engloutie*

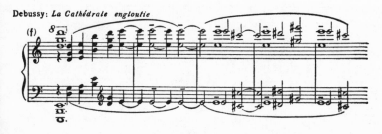

EMERGING TONAL COMPLEXITY

Ex. 3 Egon Wellesz: *Alkestis, 1923*

Schoenberg's Twelve-Tone Technique

Ex. 4 Schoenberg: String Quartet No. 4

In the foregoing example the row in its entirety is seen to permeate each group. The notes of the second chord in bar 3 of our example should be numbered 1–3–2 rather than 1–2–3.

THE TWELVE-TONE TECHNIQUE OF ALBAN BERG

Ex. 5 Berg: Violin Concerto

(d) Chorale melody

Chorale

The examples are taken from Berg's Violin Concerto, his last finished composition. This concerto, apart from its artistic value, is in a sense a historic document within the development of modern music. Written in 1935, that is at a comparatively early stage of the twelve-tone era, it constitutes in many of its parts the first, already far-reaching relaxation of the rules established by Schoenberg. The actual twelve-tone technique is to a great extent abandoned, yet its spirit is maintained and even enriched through new variants and freer ways of application.

In Ex. 5a the row which constitutes the basic structural shape of the composition is given. In Ex. 5b the concerto's opening bars are quoted. As the numbers affixed to the single notes show, the shapes are in no sense derivatives of the row. Several notes are even repeated before the twelve-tone cycle is completed: for instance, G (1) from the first bar, re-emerges in the second bar; A (5) from the second bar re-emerges in the third, etc. Thus there is no question of the row being the structural directive. The twelve-tone idea is maintained merely by the introduction of all the notes of the chromatic compass in the opening bars, with G-sharp (8) following in the fourth bar. However, it is important to observe that from a motivic point of view the whole design presents a picture of transparent logic and symmetry.

This method continues up to bar 11 (beginning of Ex. 5c) where the real twelve-tone technique takes control—at least for a while. Here the row is easily perceivable, starting from G (1) in the bass, followed by B-flat (2) and D (3) in the upper chords, F-sharp (4) again in the bass, etc. These chords, be it noted, are quite openly shaped as overtone harmonies. Then, in the fifth bar of the example the actual row is heard as a thematic unit, played by the solo violin. A few bars later—no longer quoted in our example—the violin plays the row in inversion.

The last example, 5d, quotes a much-discussed part of the work, where the melody of a Bach chorale sets in. The chorale melody is played by the solo violin which is accompanied by a viola line the beginning of which is itself taken from the chorale melody. As a second counterpoint the transposed row is heard from the bass played by the contra bassoon. The first four notes of the chorale melody correspond to the last four notes of the row, and in the sixth bar of our example the bassoon plays a part of the row in inversion. But apart from the phrases just mentioned this design is again without adherence to the row or its mirror forms and is actually not even in the twelve-tone vein.

Yet we see here the clear attempt *to blend the twelve-tone technique, that is, atonality, and tonal ideas into one unified style.* How strongly the composer wished to emphasize this intention can be seen in the fact that he introduced the chorale melody with the key signature of B-flat major, which he then notated in parenthesis, and that he later, before the entrance of the fully harmonized chorale (last bar of our example), inserted the same key signature, this time without parenthesis.

Certainly, it is not claimed that this type of structure is identical with what in another part of our study is described as pantonality. The complex interrelationships and interpenetrations of diverse and contrasting tonalities which characterize that style are not included in Berg's structural concepts. Yet a synthesis of tonal and atonal elements, as well as of formations of the twelve-tone and free type, is clearly established both in the above example and in various other sections of the same work. And this trend is strikingly continued and increased in many works of today, although their composers 'officially' still adhere to the twelve-tone label.

TWO CONTRASTING STRUCTURAL TYPES

I *Béla Bartók*

Ex. 6 Bartók: Music for String Instruments, Percussion and Celesta

142

II *Anton Webern*

Ex. 7 Webern: Five Movements for String Quartet

A Rhythmical Pattern from Strawinsky

Ex. 8 Strawinsky: L'Histoire du soldat

HINDEMITH'S POLYRHYTHM

Ex. 9 Hindemith: Piano Concerto

The example is taken from Hindemith's Concerto for Piano and Twelve Solo Instruments (*Kammermusik*, No. 2), 1924. Though it is true polyrhythm, Hindemith skilfully manages to make this feature not too much of a hurdle for the performer. In Ex. 9a especially, the conductor may, after having given the pianist his cue, happily cling to the orchestra and leave it to the pianist's own musicianship to adjust his $\frac{4}{4}$ rhythm to the regular $\frac{3}{8}$ flow of the orchestra. In the variant of Ex. 9b, with the trumpet joining in the $\frac{4}{4}$ rhythm of the piano, the situation is a shade more ticklish. But even here with a little rehearsal the balance will soon be restored, if only all the participants clearly feel the underlying eighth note beat, which is the common rhythmical denominator for both contrasting motions.

CHARLES IVES

Ex.10 Ives: *Tone Roads* No.3

This example should create a minor sensation among twelve-tone circles. For here Ives in 1915 (that is, almost a decade before Schoenberg's similar endeavour) opened one of his compositions with a clear twelve-tone theme. Moreover, he repeated it in the following group in an almost Schoenbergian manner: namely by preserving the notes of the series literally, but changing their rhythmical and metrical qualities. In the repetition only tone number 12 (C) is replaced by another note. Other voices, however, which join the twelve-tone line contrapuntally, do not adhere to the row (see score).

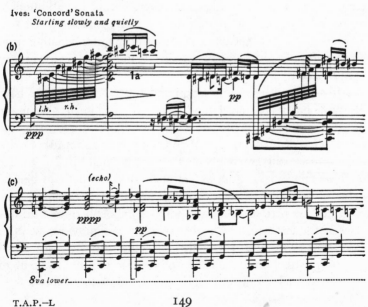

Ives: 'Concord' Sonata

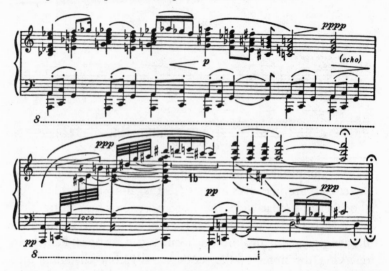

Since in the general section of this study there was little opportunity to elaborate on Ives' many novel structural ideas, a few observations may now be inserted. Naturally, the brief examples quoted above give less than an intimation of the wide range of his palette. Neither, however, would the addition of more and lengthier quotations have sufficed to convey even an approximate idea of the inner artistic atmosphere emanating from his creations. For Ives was one of the few innovators in the history of musical art.

After years of artistic isolation and frustrating efforts to have his music heard and understood, Ives, who died in 1954 at the age of eighty, now begins to attract attention.[1] However, the true importance of his achievement and the potentialities it holds for the future are still far from being fully comprehended. The essence of this achievement in an evolutional sense can perhaps best be indicated by viewing it in comparison with that of other composers of the period. The polyphony of Schoenberg and his followers, for instance, much as it may surpass previous ways of formation with regard to harmonic concepts and patterns of grouping, still remains a polyphony of single lines, even if of diversified, melodically autonomous lines. So also is Strawinsky's

[1]For authentic material on Ives see Henry and Sidney Cowell's comprehensive study *Charles Ives*, Oxford University Press, New York, 1955.

polyphonic web, which in spite of all its effects and whims of varied rhythm and colour, is still more clearly rooted in the classical example. But Ives for the first time in history establishes, or at least tries to establish, in quite a number of his compositions *a polyphony of groups*. A polyphony in which the elements are not lines but full musical entities which carry within themselves their harmonic and contrapuntal life.

In fact, almost all the other characteristic features of his style: his much discussed polyrhythm, his entirely free way of phrasing and grouping, even his frequent blending of outspokenly tonal and outspokenly atonal elements, and sometimes even his peculiar notation, are often but consequences of his concept of group polyphony. It is particularly impressive to observe how this idea of group polyphony often becomes the architectural basis not only of his gigantic formations, as for instance his Fourth Symphony, but even of some of his simplest and humblest creations, as can be seen from his composition for orchestra, *The Unanswered Question*. The strings, the winds and the solo trumpet, which here constitute three entirely divergent groups, symbolizing Man's age-old question and the world's noisy answer, are still forged into a perfect unit. Indeed, in such designs the essential problem, of which recent imitators of Ives often seem to be little aware, is whether such divergent groups can be unified in one artistic organization. In the time of Gabrieli double choirs were not faced with this difficulty. For multiplicity of groups was then in a sense an external feature, all groups still progressing on a common melodic-harmonic or quasi-harmonic ground. But in modern music, as Ives imagined it, the independence and diversity of groups goes deeper. And this diversity can only be—and is often by Ives—reconciled through those very cross-relations of 'tonalities of a higher order' which are extensively described in this study. Ives, to be sure, remained in part of his work an experimenter. In trying to realize dreams he sometimes broke the clay before he was able to mould it into the finished work. Yet at other times his genius led him far beyond mere experiment and he became a true creator of new musical beauty. Thus he reached farther into the future than others who in a technical sense may have come nearer to their goal.

Pierre Boulez' A-Thematic Serial Structure

Ex. 11 Boulez: Sonata No. 1

Benjamin Britten's 'Tonal Multitonality'

Ex.12 Britten: *The Rape of Lucretia*

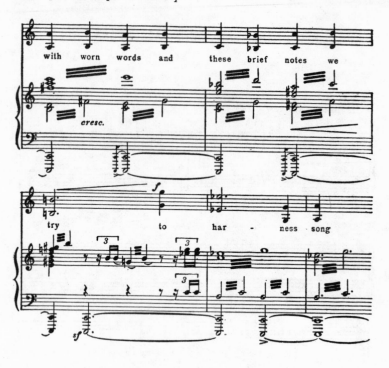

AARON COPLAND

Ex. 13 Copland: Symphony No. 3

*In the score this upper group written for trumpets in B-flat is notated in flats.

ANDRÉ JOLIVET

Ex. 14 Jolivet: Piano Concerto

(b)

(c)

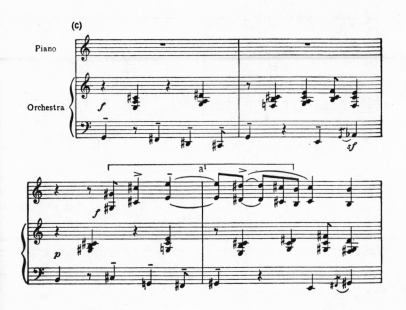

RUDOLPH RETI

Ex.15 Reti: *The Dead Mourn the Living*

Reti: Three Allegories for Orchestra

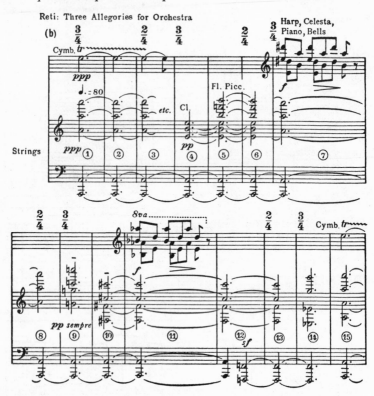

(c) basic chords inversions extensions variants

(upwards) (downwards)

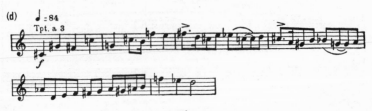

160

ACKNOWLEDGMENTS

IDELSOHN   *Jewish Music: Its Historical Development*
Copyright by Henry Holt and Company, New York.

DEBUSSY   *Reflets dans l'eau*
Autorisation Durand & Cie Editeurs propriétaires, Paris.
La Cathédrale engloutie
Autorisation Durand & Cie Editeurs propriétaires, Paris.

WELLESZ   *Alkestis*
Copyright 1923, renewed 1951, by Universal Edition, Vienna.

SCHOENBERG   *String Quartet No. 4*
Copyright 1939 by G. Schirmer, Inc., New York.

BERG   *Violin Concerto*
Copyright 1936 by Universal Edition, Vienna.

BARTÓK   *Music for Strings, Percussion and Celesta*
Copyright 1937 by Universal Edition (London) Ltd.
Copyright for the United States assigned Boosey & Hawkes Inc.

WEBERN   *Five Movements for String Quartet*
Copyright 1922, renewed 1949, by Universal Edition, Vienna.

STRAWINSKY   *L'Histoire du Soldat*
Copyright by J. W. Chester Ltd., London.

HINDEMITH   *Kammermusik No. 2.*
Copyright 1924, renewed 1952, by B. Schott's Soehne, Mainz.

ACKNOWLEDGMENTS

IVES   *Tone Roads No. 3*
>Copyright 1952 by Peer International Corporation, New York.

Piano Sonata No. 2
>Copyright 1947 by Arrow Music Press, Inc., New York.

BOULEZ   *Piano Sonata No. 1*
>By courtesy of the Amphion, Editions Musicales, Paris.

BRITTEN   *The Rape of Lucretia*
>Copyright 1946 by Boosey & Hawkes Ltd. Used by permission.

COPLAND   *Symphony No. 3*
>Copyright 1947 by Boosey & Hawkes Ltd. Used by permission.

JOLIVET   *Piano Concerto*
>Copyright 1953 by Heugel & Cie., Paris.

RETI   *The Magic Gate*
>Copyright 1957 by Broude Brothers, New York.

Acknowledgments are also due to Mrs. Gertrud Schoenberg and to Josef Matthias Hauer for the letters reproduced on Plates I and II.

INDEX

Alkestis (Wellesz), 34n, 134 *ill.*
American music, 30, 43n, 63, 89, 98, 99, 105n
Anti-romanticism, 123–5, 126
Apel, Willi, 123n
A-rhythm and pan-rhythm, 79–89, 106
Art and the time, influence of, 126–30
A-thematic music, 94–100, 106, 152 *ill.*
Atonality, 2–4, 31–55, 65, 68–9, 71, 75, 82–4, 92, 93–4, 95, 97, 100, 106, 108, 110–12, 116–18, 125, 126, 140; Schoenberg's concept of, 40, 44–5

Bach, Johann Sebastian, 1, 20, 123n, 129
Banshee, 105n
Bartók, Béla, 37, 85
    Music for Strings, Percussion and Celesta, 73–4, 76, 77–8, 93, 142–3 *ill.*
Beethoven, Ludwig van, 22, 28n, 60, 81, 123n, 124n, 129
    'Eroica' Symphony, 28n
    Piano Sonatas, 28n
Berg, Alban, 50, 72; twelve-tone technique of, 138–9 *ill.*
    Violin Concerto, 50, 138–9 *ill.*, 139–41
Berlioz, Hector, 101
Biblical chant, 15, 17, 19, 23–5, 29, 77, 133 *ill.*
Bitonality, 59–61, 64; Debussy's, 28, 60, 117
Blacher, Boris, 87
Boulez, Pierre, Piano Sonata No. 1, 96–8, 152 *ill.*
Brahms, Johannes, 1, 22, 124n
British music, developments in, 23, 30, 34, 98, 99, 110n
Britten, Benjamin, *Rape of Lucretia*, 97–8, 153–4 *ill.*
Bruckner, Anton, 33, 124n
Busoni, Ferruccio, 61
Buxtehude, Dietrich, 20

Casella, Alfredo, 64
Cathédrale engloutie, La, 29, 135 *ill.*
Chopin, Frédéric François, 60, 124n
Classical music, 4, 8–14, 16, 21–2, 29, 30, 59, 66, 80–1, 90, 91–2, 93, 101, 112

Colour in music, evolution of, 100–3
Composition with twelve tones, 35, 42–8, 108 (*see also* Twelve-tone technique)
Consonance and dissonance, 9–10, 38–40, 47, 49–50, 70–6, 86, 129–30
Copland, Aaron, 99
    Third Symphony, 98–9, 155 *ill.*
Couperin, François, 20
Cowell, Henry, 105n, 150n

Dallapiccola, Luigi, 53–4, 88
Dance music, 82
Dead Mourn the Living, The, 159 *ill.*
Debussy, Claude, 2, 59–60, 67, 77, 84, 86, 94, 117; tonality of, 22–30, 59, 62, 134–5 *ill.*
    La cathédrale engloutie, 29, 135 *ill.*
    La Mer, 102
    Reflets dans l'eau, 23–6, 134 *ill.*
Dissonance and consonance, *see* Consonance
Dissonances, gradation of, 70n
Don Giovanni (Mozart), 88n
Durand, J., 23

Electronic music, 103–7, 118, 125
Elektra (Strauss), 21
English developments, *see* British music
'Eroica' Symphony, 28n

Fetis, Joseph, 7
Folk music, 19–20, 22, 23, 29, 77
Form in music, 89–100
French music, developments in, 21, 22, 23, 30, 34, 112
Fugue, technique of, 108, 109

Gabrieli, Andrea, 151
Gelatt, Roland, 119n
George Lieder, 34
German music, developments in, 21, 22, 33, 34n
Gregorian Chant, 15–17, 19–20
Gurrelieder, 33

164